Alexandre Kojève

20TH CENTURY POLITICAL THINKERS

Series Editors:
Kenneth L. Deutsch and Jean Bethke Elshtain

Alexandre Kojève

Wisdom at the End of History

James H. Nichols, Jr.

ROWMAN & LITTLEFIELD PUBLISHERS, INC.
Lanham • Boulder • New York • Toronto • Plymouth, UK

ROWMAN & LITTLEFIELD PUBLISHERS, INC.

Published in the United States of America
by Rowman & Littlefield Publishers, Inc.
A wholly owned subsidary of The Rowman & Littlefield Publishing Group, Inc.
4501 Forbes Boulevard, Suite 200, Lanham, Maryland 20706
www.rowmanlittlefield.com

Estover Road, Plymouth PL6 7PY, United Kingdom

British Library Cataloguing in Publication Information Available

Library of Congress Cataloging-in-Publication Data

Nichols, James H., 1944-
  Alexandre Kojève : wisdom at the end of history / James H. Nichols, Jr.
    p. cm. — (20th century political thinkers)
  Includes bibliographical references and index.
  ISBN-13: 978-0-7425-2776-8 (cloth : alk. paper)
  ISBN-10: 0-7425-2776-X (cloth : alk. paper)
  ISBN-13: 978-0-7425-2777-5 (pbk. : alk. paper)
  ISBN-10: 0-7425-2777-8 (pbk. : alk. paper)
  1. Kojève, Alexandre, 1902-1968. 2. History—Philosophy. 3. Philosophy—History.
  4. Hegel, Georg Wilhelm Friedrich, 1770-1831. I. Title. II. Series.

  B2430.K654N53 2007
  194—dc22

                                                                  2007011488

Printed in the United States of America

Contents

Acknowledgments

I should like to express my gratitude to all those who have helped to provide the opportunity for me to write this book on the political thought of Alexandre Kojève. In doing this, I will necessarily recapitulate my own course of involvement with his work.

Moving from the present backward, I wish to thank Kenneth Deutsch and Jean Bethke Elshtain, the general editors of this series of books on twentieth-century political thinkers, for inviting me to contribute the book on Alexandre Kojève. I wish also to thank Claremont McKenna College for two sabbaticals that made it possible to devote my time to reading and writing about Kojève, and to thank the Gould Center for Humanistic Studies at Claremont McKenna College for a summer fellowship grant in 1999 that provided me timely and helpful assistance.

My chief involvement with the work of Alexandre Kojève before this present project was my translation of his *Introduction to the Reading of Hegel*. Allan Bloom, with whom I studied during my freshman year of college at Yale and then later in graduate school at Cornell, had kindled in me a fascination with the issues of political philosophy. It was thanks to his persuasive mentoring that, in my sophomore year, I began my study of ancient Greek and resumed Latin. At some time during that year, Irving Kristol, then publisher of Basic Books, proposed to Bloom that he prepare a translation of Kojève's *Introduction à la Lecture de Hegel*. Bloom, eager to continue uninterruptedly his work on a translation of Plato's *Republic*, told Kristol that he could recommend someone to do it: a student of political philosophy whose French was fluent and who had successfully translated, the summer before, Kojève's article "The Emperor Julian and His Art of Writing." Kristol was willing to accept that suggestion, contingent upon Bloom's taking responsibility for the project as editor.

So it came to pass that I spent the summer of 1964 in Paris, beginning to work on the translation of Kojève's book (or more precisely, about half of the book, in accordance with the publisher's decision, with the selections to be made by the editor). Now, I mention all this not only to express my indebtedness to Allan Bloom's confidence in me and my gratitude to Irving Kristol's decision to publish a translation of Kojève, but also to have an excuse to mention the lunch that I had with Alexandre Kojève. It was arranged by Allan Bloom, who at Leo Strauss's suggestion had gotten to know Kojève rather well and had studied some writings of Hegel under his guidance. The reader can well imagine that an undergraduate, halfway toward his B.A., was rather too lacking in knowledge to pose the crucial probing questions that he might now wish that he had asked. Certainly Bloom and Kojève did almost all of the talking at the lunch in question. I remember asking him whether he thought *Geist* was better translated as *mind* or *spirit* and that he opted firmly for the latter. I remember that Bloom at one point steered the conversation to Kojève's practical activities at the French Ministry of Economics and Finance, and I have a vague recollection of Kojève talking about his work as administering the end of history. I think he talked at one point about how in the ultimate universal and homogeneous state, all the world's cultural riches would have to be made equally available to all mankind; since too vast a stream of tourists would spoil the cultural experience, for example, of visiting Paris's Cathedral of Notre Dame, he supposed that some technological solution would be achieved: probably some way of transporting Notre Dame all around the world to be viewed by whoever might wish to see it. Bloom at one point commented on how impressively serious Leo Strauss was about his work, and Kojève commented, "Oui, Strauss est très humain" ("Yes, Strauss is very human"); Kojève, of course, argued that the wise man at the end of history has risen above mere humanity and become in some sense divine. The translation was eventually finished in 1968, and shortly after Bloom finished writing his "Editor's Introduction," we learned that Kojève had died at an international meeting in Brussels.

To my regret, I only met Kojève that one time, for I did not have the opportunity to spend time in Paris again until 1969–1970. During that year I was able to spend some time with people who had known Kojève—chiefly Pierre Hassner, but also on a few occasions Raymond Aron. I also attended a couple of courses at the Sorbonne from which I was able to get a bit more of a sense of the character of French intellectual life at the time (in which connection I would mention in particular the late Professor Henri Birault, from whose fascinating courses on Nietzsche and on Heidegger I learned many things of great interest, some of them very helpful to my thinking about Kojève).

To take just one more step backward, I would like to express my gratitude to those who helped me learn French, for it was my fluency in French that made it possible for Bloom to propose me as translator of Kojève (and that contributed crucially to my fondness for French life and culture, something that, along with a love of political philosophy, I shared in common with Bloom). As regards learning French, the key experience for me was the first semester of my senior year of high school that I spent on the American Field Service foreign student exchange program. I am deeply grateful to that worthy program and to two French families with whom I lived in Lyon: chiefly the family of Maurice Philip and (at the start of my stay, before the Philips returned from summer vacation) the family of Dr. Jacques Bourret.

From September to January I attended school at the Externat Sainte Marie in Lyon, where I participated in the last year of high school education, which was called (if memory serves) "l'année de philosophie" (the year of philosophy). During that year, if one chose, as I did, the option of concentrating on philosophy (rather than on mathematics or natural sciences), one took a course in philosophy that met twelve hours per week. This course had a profound effect on me; it was my first introduction to the very notion of philosophy, and I wish to express my gratitude to le Père Fournel whose learned, lively, and thoughtful teaching led me to begin to think in a serious manner about philosophical issues, as well as immersing me in (French) philosophical and moral vocabulary. My recollection of details of the course is hazy from the more than forty years of time that have since elapsed. But I think it kindled in me an interest in philosophy, and in some distinctively French aspects of thinking, that has remained alive ever since. During that semester, le Père Fournel presented a course in philosophical ethics; in retrospect, I think I could sum up his position, as best I can remember it, as an updated development of the Pascalian "misère de l'homme sans Dieu" (the misery of man without God); by "updated," I mean that he also drew deeply on arguments and insights of many later thinkers, of which I remember Nietzsche most vividly, while pointing the implications of such insights toward the Pascalian conclusion. The course kindled my interest in philosophy, gave me a sense that certain theological questions were inextricably connected to philosophy, and brought me closer than I had been before or have been since to religious experience.

After many years of inquiry into quite other matters than Kojève's thought, it has been deeply rewarding to read and reread his works, most of them posthumously published. I have come away from that experience with a sense of the greatness of his intellectual gifts and accomplishments, with a regret that his largest philosophical project remained uncompleted and that he did not find time to perfect some of his texts rhetorically so as more strongly to catch the attention of more readers, and with the expectation that scholarly awareness of the importance of his contribution to the political philosophical discussion of the twentieth century is likely to grow in the future.

Introduction

History is over. It has come to its fulfillment, its completion, its end. This seemingly paradoxical, not to say outrageous, assertion is what people are most likely to think of when they hear the name Alexandre Kojève, if they think of anything at all. And they are right to have this thought, for in its way it sums up the philosophical position that Kojève developed in the course of his life better than any other single sentence could do. As its title suggests, this book has as its central purpose to make sense of this strange assertion. What does it mean? Why was Kojève led to assert it? What are its implications for our understanding of the world, especially politics?

Alexandre Kojève exerted a powerful influence on French intellectual life in the middle third of the twentieth century, but in a rather hidden or behind-the-scenes manner. The famous seminar he taught in Paris from 1933 to 1939 on Hegel's *Phenomenology of Spirit* (explored in chapter 2 below) deeply affected a number of thinkers, some of them soon to be more widely known than he, but his publications were few, he held no regular academic post, and he rarely lectured. He also played an important but mainly hidden role in French politics, as a senior bureaucrat dealing with foreign economic relations in the French ministry of economics and finance, active especially in matters relating to the European Economic Community and GATT (the General Agreement on Tariffs and Trade, which played a powerful role in shaping the postwar world). His practical, bureaucratic, or administrative effect on some issues of fundamental importance for France and for Europe was great, but he remained very much an *éminence grise* rather than a publicly known figure.

In America, Kojève was relatively unknown, except to Hegel scholars and to students introduced to him and his thought by Leo Strauss. The book

1

consisting of notes and transcripts from his famous seminar, published by Raymond Queneau as *Introduction à la Lecture de Hegel* in 1947, made his name familiar to Hegel scholars; in America, for instance, C. J. Friederich's new introduction to a translation of Hegel's *Philosophy of History* in 1956 mentions Kojève's book as "the most remarkable book in this trend," that is, in a "Hegel Renaissance" that was taking place especially in France and Germany.[1] American readers interested in Leo Strauss became familiar with Kojève from the publication in 1963 of *On Tyranny*, Strauss's study of Xenophon's dialogue followed by a long critical essay by Kojève, entitled "Tyranny and Wisdom," and Strauss's reply. In the foreword to that book, published by the Free Press in the Agora Series of which he was general editor, Allan Bloom plausibly enough referred to Kojève at that time as "virtually unknown in America."[2]

A quarter-century after his death in 1968, however, Kojève's name came to the fore in discussions among a much wider circle in America thanks to the publication of Francis Fukuyama's article "The End of History?"[3] This article took Kojève's best-known thesis, that history has come to its end or fulfillment, and applied it to the contemporary world. Published in a hitherto rather obscure journal, the article provoked such abundant and widespread discussion that the names of Hegel and even of Kojève were on the lips of many a columnist, political intellectual, and foreign policy maker. It is worth noting about this intellectual event (renewed with the publication of Fukuyama's book-length sequel)[4] that virtually everyone who weighed in on the discussion found it necessary emphatically to reject the Kojèvean argument that history had come to an end. Often the rejection was based on a misinterpretation of the Fukuyama/Kojève thesis, as though it maintained the patent absurdity that "the end of history" meant that political events or military confrontations or any other happenings of interest would suddenly stop. Other critics, however, avoiding that simple misinterpretation, raised a great many other objections, some of them containing more evident common sense than the thesis itself would appear at first sight to have. But why did so many people feel called upon to make the effort to address a thesis that almost everyone considers to be so evidently wrong and contrary to common sense?

A first answer to that question must surely have to do with the character of the times. After all, Kojève's Hegelian end of history argument had been available for fifty years and had for a time incited substantial intellectual ferment but without provoking anything like so broad a public discussion. But now the Berlin Wall had come down, the Soviet Union was falling into pieces, and the Western democracies led by the United States of America seemed to have won a decisive victory over the last powerful alternative to the liberal democratic way of life. Surely the key difference was the quality of the moment: specific current events made the thesis, however paradoxical in itself, much more plausibly applicable to the world than it had ever seemed before.

However circumstances might make it seem more plausible, the thesis remains an odd one in itself, and still more so as attributed to Hegel by Kojève. To many it seemed quite strange to evoke Hegelian philosophy in order to argue for an end of history characterized by the triumph of liberal democracies, for Hegel had offered many criticisms of liberalism (presented in most detail in his *Philosophy of Right*) as too abstract and as humanly and politically incomplete. Kojève had already articulated his own difference from Hegel's explicit political analysis of the end of history through his description of it as the coming of the "universal and homogeneous state." (He works out these political and juridical revisions of Hegel most fully in his *Outline of a Phenomenology of Right*, which I examine in chapter 3). Others found it particularly ironical to evoke Kojève's end of history in the context of the late twentieth century, since Kojève was, notoriously, a Marxist kind of Hegelian who had expressed admiration for the Soviet Union and even presented himself as ready to justify Stalin's actions, whereas Fukuyama's end of history seemed especially to capture the moment by celebrating liberalism's victory over communism. Here too, however, Kojève himself had in fact paved the way. In the late thirties and early forties, he had indeed drawn Marxist or even Marxist-Leninist conclusions about the political situation and justified Stalin's program, but by the mid-fifties, he had revised his thinking on that point and held to a thoroughgoing convergence theory, elaborated and specified with the additional claim that the United States was much further along toward the "Marxist" end of history than the Soviets. This revision in Kojève's thinking is explored in chapter 4 below.

Beyond the events of the moment, however, something deeper is involved as well. The strange thesis about the end of history, while accepted by almost no one, does nonetheless give voice to a powerful strand in the thinking of many people for the last two centuries. One can see this point most simply by reflecting on the fact that most people believe, one way or another, in progress. They believe one historical epoch is essentially different from another, that fundamental change takes place in the world, and that historical change is overall for the better. People do not typically assert that historical progress is over; indeed, more typically they suppose that progress is an unending task, to use Kant's famous phrase. But most people believe in the reality of fundamental change for the better so deeply that they normally take it absolutely for granted that any wish to return to an earlier day and age is impossible or, if possible, would be folly. A very ordinary expression of this deep underlying belief is to call something out of date. Of all possible labels, the devastating "out of date" most effectively prevents anything so labeled from being taken seriously. (In *The Notion of Authority*, Kojève illustrates the authority of the present through the phrase, which he gives in English, of wanting to be "up to date" as well as the phrase not wanting "to be behind the times," for which he gives the French expression "en retard sur son temps."[5]) The rational force of Kojève's thesis can be seen most readily if one asks, "How can I know that historical change is or has been for the better?" If one were, say, an Aristotelian, one could articulate and defend, based on reasoning about nature and experience, a conception of the highest good for human beings—a good whose perfection doubtless puts it mostly out of reach of full attainment, but the effort to attain which provides reasonable guidance to human action. On that basis, one could then speak of changes (political, ethical, intellectual) as moving toward or away from the best state. But Aristotelians hold to a permanent primacy of unchanging nature; they do not believe that human beings (or any other beings, for that matter) radically or fundamentally change in history. So if, unlike Aristotelians and all other such thinkers, we believe, in accordance with the modern (Hegelian and post-Hegelian) view, that historical change is fundamental or essential, how can we know that history has made progress unless we know its goal? And if history is a free and contingent process (as Kojève's variant of the Hegelian view of history also holds), rather than something determined by God or some eternal necessity, how can we be sure that change for the better has taken place unless we know the process as a whole, that is, unless history is over?

In short, the curious fact that a broad public discussion arose concerning the possibility of the end of history can be understood both as a response to particular circumstances and as linked to a fundamental conviction about progress. This conviction is customarily held without serious testing and examination, but raising the question about the end of history called forth a fuller awareness of people's attachment to that conviction and stirred up interest in the debate. One could even go further, as Leo Strauss had done in debate with Kojève in the 1950s, to assert that Kojève's position is the clearest and most far-reaching elaboration of the character and end of modern rationalism. In Strauss's formulation, on the one hand ancient philosophers like Plato and Aristotle hold that human being, human discourse, and human history exist and develop within an eternal framework of nature, to which our search for genuine knowledge must always ultimately refer. By contrast, the culmination of the modern approach as articulated by Kojève holds that human beings (and indeed Being itself as accessible to discursive philosophic reasoning) create themselves in the course of history. Both of these approaches, to which Kojève would apply the labels pagan and Christian, respectively, resonate deeply with different aspects of people's thinking. This resonance and the divination that something fundamental about our mode of being in the world was at stake brought it about that the question of the end of history found eager discussants.

So far in these introductory remarks, I have tried to suggest the importance of Kojève's political thought by sketching his fundamental position both as especially relevant to our current circumstances and as one of the fundamental philosophic alternatives. A brief survey of some aspects of Kojève himself will serve to complete this preliminary argument for the importance of his thought. Let me begin with what is easiest of access, the judgments of other people who have some plausible claim to be taken as authorities. Three in particular—Raymond Aron, Leo Strauss, and Jacob Klein—disagreed with Kojève's political stance and fundamental philosophical position, but nonetheless considered him to be one of the most, or even the most, brilliant and intelligent people whom they had known personally. Raymond Aron, for instance, described him as "the most intelligent man I ever knew."[6]

Secondly, Kojève is of unusual interest to students of political thought in that he was both a political philosopher (to speak from a skeptical standpoint, for Kojève himself claims, with Hegel, to have moved from philosophy to a complete system of definitive knowledge or wisdom) and a practical active statesman, in the appropriately Hegelian mode of a bureaucrat. While this combination has certainly existed before, in persons like Cicero, Francis Bacon, and John Locke, it seems to be something much more exceptional in the twentieth century. Accordingly, a recent book has persuasively asserted of Kojève that it is "difficult to think of a significant European thinker of the last century who played an equivalent role in the shaping of European politics, or a statesman with comparable philosophical ambitions."[7]

Most importantly, Kojève's writings reveal him to be a thinker of vast learning, with a comprehensive knowledge rarely to be found at any time, and almost never in contemporary times. A philosopher like Aristotle, or even a philosopher as late as Hegel, could not unreasonably claim competent familiarity with the most important achievements in every area of human knowledge. This impressive human type, exemplified perhaps as well by Leonardo da Vinci as by anyone, even acquired among us a nickname, "Renaissance man." Given the immense amount of progress in every kind of science and learning over the past two hundred years, no one, it seems, can any longer make the kind of claim that could still be advanced for Hegel. Kojève himself certainly never states any such claim for himself. I am nevertheless inclined to say that he comes closer to approximating that kind of comprehensive knowledge than anyone else I can think of in the twentieth century.

The most massive difficulty that confronts our human desire for comprehensive knowledge today arises from what C. P. Snow called the problem of the two cultures. The natural sciences, and most notably the foundational science of physics, have developed so far and so fast, and on so difficult a mathematical basis, that they have become deeply separated from philosophy, history, and the other human sciences. But can there possibly be a comprehensive philosophical argument in isolation from physics? Kojève himself explicitly denies it, in a noteworthy passage from his book on Kant: "Every Philosopher must take account and give an account of the *Physics* of his time, even if he rejects the supposedly 'philosophical' ideas of *Physicists* in general and of contemporary Physicists in particular."[8] Kojève is that rare exception: someone who followed closely the latest advances in physics (both Einstein's relativity and, what he considered most importantly new, the quantum physics of Planck, Heisenberg, and others). He pursued this knowledge of physics not just from the outside, by reading simplified accounts for the general public of scientific advances, but by serious study. In the twenties, he sought private tutoring in tensor calculus from a Russian mathematician so that he could adequately understand Einstein's theories, and he read the great breakthrough articles of Planck, Heisenberg, and others in quantum physics. (His book *The Idea of Determinism in Classical Physics and in Modern Physics*, discussed in chapter 1 below, is his most substantial writing on natural science.) It is Kojève's knowledge of physics, as we shall see, that led him, though never ceasing to describe himself as Hegelian, to take a different position from Hegel in one altogether fundamental respect.

In other respects as well, Kojève's learning was vast. His knowledge of philosophy was assisted by most impressive linguistic accomplishments. Writings by him have come down to us in Russian, German, and French. He studied and used for his philosophical self-education ancient Greek, Latin, Sanskrit, Chinese, and Tibetan. His interest in religion, including Eastern religions, was keen and pursued with scholarly depth. He wrote a fascinating sketch of the history of art and its culmination in the type of art developed by his uncle, Wassily Kandinsky, and their correspondence shows Kandinsky's keen interest in Kojève's artistic judgment. He wrote about contemporary literature, and his broad reading in older literature reveals itself in frequent literary examples that illustrate his philosophical arguments.

This book seeks to explore the character and the importance of Kojève's political thought. Since Kojève himself argues that Hegel completed the evolution of philosophy in the decisive respects and so in his system transformed philosophy or love of wisdom into knowledge or wisdom itself, one interesting approach to Kojève would seek to understand and to evaluate him as an interpreter of Hegel. That approach, suitable to scholarly concern with Hegel himself, is not the one taken here. Rather, my effort is to understand Kojève's own thought. Certain comparisons with the thought of Hegel are of course unavoidable, since Kojève's thought is Hegelian, to be sure, as he never tires of announcing. But my effort here is not to assess the accuracy of his interpretation of Hegel, but the character and worth of Kojève's own thought. This approach seems especially appropriate in that, while Kojève himself considered Hegel the great completer of philosophic development in the key respect of understanding man and the possibility of discursive wisdom, he also considered Hegel's position untenable as regards the science of nature. And for this reason, Kojève also found it necessary to take an ontologically dualist position, in fundamental contrast with Hegel's monism.

With its focus on exploring his political thought, this book does not attempt to provide a biography of Kojève. This choice is made with no intention or implication of belittling biography nor of denying that biography can be of great value in assisting one to comprehend a difficult author's thought. But Dominique Auffret has published a long and well-researched biography,[9] and without trying to write another biography, I draw on his account when in my judgment biographical facts are especially helpful for explaining some aspect of Kojève's writing.

This book chiefly follows the order in which Kojève wrote, and therefore it begins, in chapter 1, with writings on his first philosophical concerns, religion and physics. Kojève wrote his doctoral thesis on the religious thought of Vladimir Soloviev, which he restated more briefly for publication in French in the early thirties. His first work that he himself considered important, though uncompleted, is the book *Atheism*; it is dated by its author October 14, 1931, and is now his second most recently published posthumous work. Also in the thirties he wrote the book *The Idea of Determinism in Classical Physics and in Modern Physics* (dated 1932), in which he explored at length and in depth the philosophical basis of classical physics' principle of determinism and its radical change with the advent of quantum physics. From these early writings, we see a thinker absorbed in reflection on two great questions. On the one hand, what is man's relation to what is outside the world of his concrete spatial-temporal experience, that is, to something other; and is that something other best understood as God or as nothingness? On the other hand, how do we come to know the objective reality of the physical world outside of us, what presuppositions underlie our search for valid science, and how does one or another approach to science relate to our quest for comprehensive discursive knowledge?

Chapter 2 deals with what is arguably the key intellectual development in Kojève's life: his attaining an understanding of, coming to terms with, and making his own the Hegelian philosophy, as he came to understand it in the course of teaching his famous seminar on *The Phenomenology of Spirit* from 1933 to 1939. His insights into Hegelian philosophy during this period appear to have put together for him, in a definitive way, approaches to the several deepest questions that had occupied his thinking up to that point in his life. However that may be, without a doubt this seminar was the most important source of Kojève's intellectual impact on his contemporaries, many of whom have passed down vivid descriptions of the amazing impact of Kojève's teaching.

Kojève's interpretation of Hegel in his seminar on *The Phenomenology of Spirit* is notable for its announcement of the end of history. But what exactly does that mean, and what are the actual political and juridical details of an end of history characterized as the coming of the universal and homogeneous state? Furthermore, how are we likely to move from the situation today toward the universal and homogeneous state? Chapter 3 addresses these questions through the examination of three texts, all written during the war but published only posthumously. The most recently published work, *La Notion de l'Autorité*, written in 1942 and published in 2004, provides a broad and in some sense comprehensive analysis of the fundamental four types of authority and how they are combined in various kinds of political orders. The largest single volume, Kojève's *Outline of a Phenomenology of Right*, written in 1943 and published in 1980, is his most detailed phenomenological and historical reflection on right, law, justice, and their relation to the state. Finally, a forty-page manuscript written in 1945 and published in 1990, "L'Empire Latin: Esquisse d'une doctrine de la politique française (1945)"[10] explains the end of the nation-state and explores the coming transition, through a period dominated by empires that are larger than nation-states, toward the universal and homogeneous state.

In chapter 4, the precise character and status of the end of history is pursued in more detail. Right after the war, Kojève restated his more or less Marxist stance on the end of history. Within a few years, however, he changed his mind: the end of history was not a future goal toward which one still needed to strive through a program of political action; rather, Hegel got it right in the first place. History really did end in 1806. Subsequent events are not world historical politics, for the essential political historical evolution and the great political revolutions are over. What remains—and what has been going on since Hegel correctly announced the end of history—is but the working out of administrative details. Once a wholehearted Stalinist, Kojève now elaborated the view that, in fact, the United States had advanced further along the path of actualizing the Hegelian-Marxist end of history than the Soviet Union. And like Heidegger, Kojève found no fundamental difference between the United States and the Soviet Union, but held to a thoroughgoing convergence theory. During this same time (the fifties), Kojève's writings raise and reflect on the problem of the character of human life at the end of history.

What is the character of human life, what are human possibilities, when the great creative tasks of historical evolution have been completed? Kojève articulated the possibility that posthistorical life could involve the loss of humanity or a return to animality (rather in the manner of Nietzsche's "last man"), but he also considered the possibility (which the example of Japan brought home to him) that a formalistic posthistorical negativity could sustain the human difference from the rest of the given world.

In the fifties, Kojève spent weekends and other free time working on his philosophical writings, which he habitually referred to as his posthumous writings. These works attempt to restate and to modify as needed, so as to bring up to date, Hegel's system of knowledge. This work is unfinished; what we have is five volumes that serve to provide an introduction to the updating of Hegel's system of knowledge. The first volume, *The Concept, Time, and Discourse*, provides an overall introduction to Kojève's philosophical endeavor and two introductions to the Hegelian identification of the concept with time: a psychological introduction taking off from Aristotle and a logical introduction taking off from Plato. The three volumes of his *Attempt at a Reasoned History of Pagan Philosophy* provide the first half of the third, or historical, introduction to the Hegelian system. The second half should, of course, be an *Attempt at a Reasoned History of Christian Philosophy*; what we have in its place is only one volume, on Kant, who for Kojève is the greatest figure in the history of Christian philosophy. In chapter 5 I present some brief reflections on this most extensive of Kojève's philosophical projects.

Finally, in chapter 6 I seek to draw some conclusions about contested aspects of Kojève's thought. How, in the final analysis, should one understand his claim to be a follower of Hegel's philosophy? Given the problems about what human life would be like at the end of history, brought to our attention by Kojève's own statements, how should his position ultimately be understood? Did he, as some have claimed, work out the Hegelian rationalist position for himself, come to a clearly unsatisfactory position or dead end, and turn into a postmodern ironist? Or was he, as Strauss took him to be in their famous debate, a thoroughly and genuinely rationalist modern philosopher? And of course, in itself and for us, the most important issue of all: what if anything is the present value to us of Kojève's political thought? Is it possible to entertain seriously his claim to expound the finally valid approach to rational thinking? What are the most important grounds for skepticism about his claim? And if one is skeptical about his claim, what, if anything, can one gain of value for one's own thinking from the study of Kojève's writings?

In the epilogue, I discuss a French government agency report, summarized by the newspaper *Le Monde* in 1999, that Kojève had been for thirty years a KGB agent. Questions arising from reflection on this recent news provide an opportunity to revisit issues about the relationship of Kojève's political philosophy to political action in general and his own political action in particular.

NOTES

1. Georg Wilhelm Friedrich Hegel, *The Philosophy of History*, trans. J. Sibree (New York: Dover Publications, Inc., 1956).

2. Leo Strauss, *On Tyranny*, revised and enlarged (New York: The Free Press of Glencoe, 1963), vi.

3. Francis Fukuyama, "The End of History?" *The National Interest* (Summer 1989): 3–18.

4. Francis Fukuyama, *The End of History and the Last Man* (New York: The Free Press, 1992).

5. *Authority*, 120.

6. Raymond Aron, *The Committed Observer*, trans. James and Marie McIntosh (Chicago: Regnery Gateway, 1983), 59.

7. Mark Lilla, *The Reckless Mind: Intellectuals in Politics* (New York: New York Review of Books Press, 2001), 116.

8. *Kant*, 187.

9. Dominique Auffret, *Alexandre Kojève: La philosophie, l'Etat, la fin de l'Histoire* (Paris: Editions Grasset & Fasquelle, 1990).

10. Published in the first issue of *La Règle du Jeu* in 1990.

Chapter One

Religion, Atheism, and Physics

Kojève's youthful philosophical interests first found detailed expression in his work on religious philosophy. His doctoral dissertation, in German, dealt with the religious philosophy of Vladimir Soloviev, and some years later he published a long article in French on that topic. In 1931 he wrote, in Russian, a manuscript entitled *Atheism*; it has been translated into French by Nina Ivanoff and published quite recently (1998). While still studying religious philosophy and the languages (Sanskrit, Chinese, and Tibetan) that he found necessary for his inquiries into Eastern religions, Kojève also pursued his interest in contemporary physics, to the point of seeking tutoring in tensor calculus from a Russian mathematician in Paris in order to understand Einstein's theories adequately. His manuscript from 1932, *L'Idée du déterminisme dans la physique classique et la physique moderne* (*The Idea of Determinism in Classical Physics and in Modern Physics*, published in 1990), presents his understanding of the fundamental approaches that classical and modern (above all quantum) physics take toward their object of study. These writings do not yet give full expression to a decidedly and definitively Hegelian philosophical position, but each in some way points toward the Hegelian philosophy that Kojève would soon afterward make his own.

The long, two-part article "La Métaphysique religieuse de Vladimir Soloviev" ("The Religious Metaphysics of Vladimir Soloviev") was published in 1934–1935;[1] it draws on the work that Kojève did for his doctoral dissertation, completed in 1925 under the direction of Karl Jaspers. Kojève takes Soloviev to be a profoundly religious man, whose thinking rests most fundamentally on his own personal religious experience of God. At the same time he was deeply influenced by Hegel and above all Schelling in elaborating a kind of Christian metaphysics and historical account of the world.

Kojève's discussion of Soloviev emphasizes the religious basis; he takes with full seriousness Soloviev's accounts of his profoundly personal, mystical experience of God, especially in the form or person of *Sophia*. Soloviev tries to articulate a metaphysics that is fully compatible with his orthodox Christian faith; in doing so he draws heavily, often without specifically citing them, on Schelling and Hegel. Kojève provides a systematic and well-ordered exposition and analysis of Soloviev's doctrine, trying sympathetically to clarify his purposes and to highlight what is most interesting or profound in his writings; at the same time, he points out aspects of the writings where in his judgment Soloviev leaves problems unresolved or takes positions that stand in contradiction to what he says elsewhere.

Among the points of Soloviev's doctrine that Kojève emphasizes, he holds that the keystone of the arch of Soloviev's thinking is the teaching of *Théandrie* (the belief in Man/God, or the doctrinal belief that God is also Man). Some form of this, of course, is the distinctive and basic Christian belief, and for Soloviev this is the link between his teaching about the uni-total Absolute (God as three persons realizing supreme good, absolute truth, and perfect beauty) and his teaching about the World. Of particular importance for him is the person of Sophia, the particular aspect of God that Soloviev experienced mystically on three occasions. According to Kojève: "Soloviev attributes to the Man of Man-God ('uni-total Man,' 'ideal Humanity,' or 'free and independent Content of the Absolute') the mystical name of *Sophia* (Σοφία), the 'Wisdom of God.' And this name for him is neither metaphor nor abstract term, but the proper name of a concrete and living person."

Soloviev's doctrine of the world is a teaching about how man (who under the aspect of Eternity is somehow also *Sophia*) freely chose to separate from God, fell, and thus brought it about that the world's history is the progressive return to God. The doctrine as a whole, in Kojève's judgment, is fraught with antinomies, most fundamentally the problem of relating the eternal to the spatial-temporal. God is Man, eternally, somehow; yet Eternal Man (= *Sophia*) chooses to separate from God, which causes the temporal world to come into being and leads him to be a spatial-temporal being who therefore can and does have a history. But how that spatial-temporal being relates to the eternal cannot be discursively elaborated in a satisfactory manner. Kojève formulates it this way: "Without any doubt there exists an antinomy within the metaphysics that we are studying: the antinomy implied by the notion of becoming on the part of a being that eternally *is* what it is, by the notion of the progressive uniting in time of that which is already united from all eternity" ("The Religious Metaphysics of Vladimir Soloviev," 129).

Another expression of the fundamental antinomy arises in connection with the notion of liberty, the "fundamental antinomy implied by the idea of the liberty of an evolution whose outcome is predetermined from all eternity" ("The Religious Metaphysics of Vladimir Soloviev," 145). Soloviev insists on the free nature of the act by which (eternal) *Sophia* turns away from (eternal) God, and the free acts by which progressively *Sophia* as Soul of the World returns to God, and similarly with the freedom of human acts in the temporal world away from or toward God (by Adam, by people accepting or rejecting salvation through Christ, etc.). But at the same time, he knows (through faith) what the final outcome will be, namely the full return of Man/*Sophia* to God in an eternal harmony. But, according to Kojève, there can be no coherent explanation of "how one can foresee the character and the final result of *future* real evolution" ("The Religious Metaphysics of Vladimir Soloviev," 131). Or stated a bit more fully:

> Soloviev, who always underlines the contingency and the liberty of the Soul's acts that realize themselves in the evolution of the universe, ought to have abstained from predicting the future of that evolution. But the notions of eternal Man-God and of Christ-Savior of the world necessarily led him to affirm that the world, or the fallen Soul, would end up attaining its perfection by becoming perfect *Sophia* once again. ("The Religious Metaphysics of Vladimir Soloviev," 147)

As we shall see, problems regarding knowledge of the future play no small role in Kojève's own later reflections on the crucial issue of the end of history.

The unresolved contradictions or at least antinomies that Kojève found in Soloviev's account could be understood as constituting one of the important motivations that led Kojève later to develop a thoroughly atheistic Hegelianism, which eliminates all mystical and transcendent elements in giving a fully discursive account of the whole historical evolution of man. In a concluding evaluation of Soloviev's thought, Kojève notes that Soloviev uses Schelling's philosophical language and doctrines to articulate his own position; and Kojève suggests that the Schellingian borrowings in fact augment the contradictions in Soloviev's exposition. He suggests that what is distinctively Soloviev's as compared to Schelling's thought is a general tendency "to attribute to man a liberty, an independence, and an importance that are greater than any other thinkers, including Schelling, attributed to him" ("The Religious Metaphysics of Vladimir Soloviev," 150). One could say that Kojève's eventual atheistic Hegelianism takes what he sees as distinctively Solovievian, radicalizes it, and develops a coherent discourse free of the antinomies that he found in Soloviev, in part by expelling any reliance on access to the eternal or transcendent. Alternatively, one could say that Kojève, himself moving toward a Marxist Hegelianism, found in Soloviev a tendency congenial to himself.

On his manuscript on atheism, only recently published (1998) under the title *L'Athéisme*,[2] Kojève wrote the statement that it is unfinished and therefore should not be published. It is nonetheless of considerable interest as an expression of his philosophic inquiries prior to his becoming the Hegelian for which he is chiefly known. He begins from an examination of the possibility of atheist religion, which he finds exemplified in Buddhism. The interest in Buddhism goes back to his earliest impulse to develop his own philosophical thinking, in a youthful project to develop a "philosophy of the in-existent."[3] From his concern with Buddhism, of course, it follows necessarily that he distinguishes religion and theism. Religion is, or gives expression to, the fundamental dissatisfaction with this spatial-temporal world that we experience and the search for genuine satisfaction elsewhere, in some Other World or Beyond or even a state of nothingness. Theism, of course, is the belief or conviction that there is one (or several) superior entity (or entities) higher than the beings experienced in this world. Kojève's manuscript explores all kinds of questions regarding people's experience of divinity and others' failure to have such experience or their determination to reject it. He develops in considerable detail, and reflects in depth on, a number of ways in which the total experience of the theist's being in the world differs from that of the atheist (in language suggestive of strong interest in Husserl and still more in Heidegger). He explores the ways in which experience of the divine is given to us, and what it means not to have such experience, to deny the possibility of such experience, to assert that such experience is illusory. The conception of God is the conception of a being, a something, that is not an object in this world of our ordinary spatial-temporal experience; God is different from all the beings in this world. For the theist, this God is a something, of which he has a theistic intuition; accordingly he finds in himself something (in the Western tradition generally called the soul) that can relate to what is not of this world. For the atheist, who negates the theistic intuition, that which is outside the world and differs from all the beings in the world is nothing, and there is nothing within one to sustain a relation to the nothingness not of this world.

One's experience of what is not a thing given in this world is closely tied to (perhaps originates out of, or even is) one's way of foreseeing one's own death. We all know that upon our death we are no longer what we were in the world. What, then, is one when one is dead? (And where, if anywhere, is one?) This question occurs to all human beings, and the theist and atheist respond differently to it. The theist, taking himself to be related to the God who is outside this worldly reality, expects that he himself (or rather, his outside-the-world self that is somehow also in the world, his soul) will endure after death, in closer proximity to God. The atheist takes his death to be the final moment, beyond which he is nothing, since there is nothing outside the world to which he could be transported or to which he could sustain any relation. In fact, Kojève suggests that one cannot know for certain whether one is theist or atheist until one's experience of death:

> As I have already said, until his own death man does not know what he is, where he is; in fact he never knows until the end what theism and atheism are. Like all knowledge, this one is imperfect because it is not completed (*achevée*) (and cannot be completed). Such a self-understanding is on the one hand the completion of the atheistic (or theistic) life in the atheistic (or theistic) world, and on the other hand it is a true philosophy of atheism (or of theism) that is nothing other than the givenness to himself of man living the full life as atheist (or theist). It is the ideal. (*L'Athéisme*, 279n218)

Assuming that Kojève was already himself an atheist, as he describes himself unambiguously just a bit later, it is worth pondering the significance of his taking religion, religious thought, and personal religious experience with such evident seriousness. In this regard Kojève is quite different from an older type of atheist. I think especially of the Epicurean, who viewed religious beliefs as delusions, and disturbing and painful ones at that; one's reasonable effort is to tear out such beliefs by the roots,[4] so as to be able to see the truth of the way things really are and to experience those genuine pleasures that are compatible with that truth. For Kojève as atheist, religious belief is not true. But, as he often says later, *errare est humanum*: to err is human. That is to say, human being is fundamentally characterized by negativity, and human negativity is a rejection of the real world as it is, in at least some crucial respect. The religious experience is a crucial manifestation of that negativity: it is a rejection of satisfaction with this world, and as such it points toward something other. When that other is first stated, and if that other is asserted to exist in reality, the statement is in fact error. Error thus gives voice to human negativity, and the ideas erroneously formed and put forth can become truths when men act freely and creatively so as to transform the world and thus make former errors true. (In fact, Kojève later formulates the point epigrammatically: "Every *truth* in the proper sense of the term is an *error* that has been *corrected*".[5]) Religious experience, in other words, as a manifestation of human negativity, has to do with what is most profoundly human, even though as religious it is not adequately stated discursively, philosophically.

However much one supposes Kojève to be an atheist, since he proclaimed himself to be such in the course of developing his interpretation of Hegel's *Phenomenology of Spirit* in the seminar which began about two years after he completed this manuscript on atheism (and which is the subject of our next chapter), it is worth emphasizing that, as the passage I just quoted implies, he did not yet announce the truth of atheism over theism in this book on atheism. On the contrary, the whole book elaborates both different modes of being in the world, and treats the theistic intuition and experience of self and the world in no respect less seriously than the atheistic. In fact, Laurent Bibard, in his "Présentation" of Kojève's text, observes that Kojève himself here appears suspended between the two alternatives and equally open to both theism and atheism; indeed Bibard makes the fascinating suggestion that after Kojève's exclusively atheistic thinking represented by his seminar on Hegel and *Introduction to the Reading of Hegel*, in his later work in the 1950s on the *System of Knowledge*, he reopened the case for the need to take seriously a theistic anthropology along with the atheistic one for which he is known.

However that may be, Kojève's deep and sympathetic interest in theism and in religion may well reflect the undeniable fact that religion, even if not philosophically true, can have great power to change the world.[6] It is also the case, as Kojève states it later, in the last year of his seminar, that, until the final adequate philosophy, "real cultural or historical life, as well as its theological transposition, are always richer than the Philosophy that that life engenders."[7] Religion's pointing elsewhere than toward the present reality of the world can, to be sure, "disarm" men (to use a well-known phrase of Machiavelli's), cause them to look for satisfaction not in this world but elsewhere, and teach them resignation to the shortcomings of the world; but it can also bring forth or become a project that guides human action to change that world. Kojève suggests that even modern science owes its coming into being to Christianity. The pagan world saw eternal nature as authoritative for us. Under the influence of Christianity, man is the highest element in God's creation and is akin to God: neither the moon nor even the superlunary regions have any divine status; God while unchangeably eternal, omniscient, and omnipotent even takes on human form for the sake of mankind. And so, only in a Christian world could one conceive of the project of conquering nature for the relief of man's estate and pursuing the goal of a complete human explanation of all the works of nature.[8]

This linkage by Kojève of religion to science leads me on to the remaining work that I wish to discuss in this chapter, the book *L'Idée du déterminisme dans la physique classique et dans la physique moderne* (*The Idea of Determinism in Classical Physics and in Modern Physics*). Kojève wrote this manuscript, dated 1932 but not published until 1990, with a view to presenting it as a thesis in the history of science for a doctorate, but that plan did not come to fruition. The book begins by elaborating the character of classical physics (that of Newton, Laplace, Maxwell, etc.) and its idea of determinism, whose classic formulation is Laplace's theorem: that by the laws of physics, if one could know everything about the location and motion of every body in the universe, one could correctly calculate what all their future motions must be (and what all their past motions must have been). Kojève explores this idea in depth, asking a number of probing questions: What is really presupposed by proceeding on such a basis? What must the world be, and what must we as knowers be, in order that this determinism should make sense? Kojève shows how unsupported that classical notion of determinism is either by adequate reasoning or by experience. The principle of determinism, to be adequately supported, would require the appropriate type of completed metaphysics that would establish the necessarily deterministic character of all physical objects, but in fact physics is supported by no such metaphysics. It would also require experimental confirmation by observations of ever-increasing precision, so that one could reasonably believe that ever more precise knowledge could be obtained with ever more precise observations. After all, a defining characteristic of classical physics, as compared to the competing metaphysical theories of nature (Aristotelian, Democritean, and the like) that it sought to replace, is the demand that theory be tested by real experiments; physics should not deal in entities that cannot be tested. In fact, experimental confirmation aiming at the underlying premise of determinism is unavailable. (Kojève does not, of course, mean that classical physics lacked experimental confirmation. It had in fact much confirmation of various particular theories and applications; but it had not confirmed experimentally, nor did it even have a program of pursuing experimental confirmation of, its fundamental belief in strict causal determination.)

The theoretical posture of classical physics, according to Kojève, displays a lack of philosophical self-awareness and leaves much to be desired on account of its abstractness and incompleteness. Even before the coming of quantum physics, classical physics could have subjected its fundamental premise to the following critique. Physics spoke of the observer making ever more precise measurements of the objects, without limit, so as to move ever closer to the theoretical ideal stated by the theorem of Laplace. But when the observer measures the physical object, must he not interact with it somehow? And must not that interaction affect the motion of the object observed? If so, how can there be no limit to the precision of the abstract observer's measurement of the abstract object? Or, to put it another way, the stance of classical physics was to treat the physicist as an abstract thinking being making observations of objects that exist and follow causal laws unaffected by being observed. This in fact is an abstraction contrary to fact: the real concrete situation is a physical observer and a physical object being observed, and for both of them the process of making observations and being observed, respectively, is necessarily an interaction.

The great difference of modern physics from classical, in Kojève's view, lies in the way it conceives of the physical object and the physical observer, in such a way that it necessarily abandons Laplace's theorem (which itself underlay the whole approach of classical physics). Kojève is keenly aware that he is writing (before 1932) within close proximity to the intellectual events in physics that he is analyzing; he therefore expresses his views with a certain degree of caution and, for example, refers to his analysis as provisional and needing to be confirmed or altered in the light of subsequent developments in physics. He notes that a widely used German textbook of physics, published in 1923, referred to modern physics as distinguished from the classical as being that of Lorentz, Einstein, and Planck. According to Kojève's analysis, however, Lorentz and Einstein belong to the tradition of classical physics; in particular, Einstein's relativity, which in certain ways could seem decisively different from classical physics, should in fact properly be understood as its final perfecting stage.

The truly different, modern physics is the quantum physics of Planck, Bohr, Schrödinger, Heisenberg, De Broglie, and others, which has made it necessary to take a different view of the fundamental nature of deterministic causality and of the nature of the conduct of physics. From a Hegelian standpoint, it is of particular interest that physics no longer represents its activity to itself quite as abstractly as it once did. (Hegel had criticized Newtonian physics for its intellectual abstractness.) The new physics no longer speaks of an abstract observer, situated God knows where, observing, measuring, and knowing the physical objects without affecting them. Now, in fact, the interaction between physical observer and physical objects observed is a part of physics; and it is not just a discursive critique directed against physics from the outside (as was Hegel's), but physics itself has uncovered its own necessity to deal with the concrete interaction, and it has even been quantified by Heisenberg and so brought into the normal activity of (the new) physics itself. Hegel criticized earlier modern philosophy for the abstractness both of the thinking subject and of the isolated things thought; as Kojève put it later, the concrete reality is spirit, or subject-knowing-the-object (= object-known-by-the-subject) or reality-revealed-by-speech (= speech-revealing-reality). Somewhat similarly now, physics is no longer the isolated abstract knower observing the thing in itself (which is not accessible to physics) or the abstract isolated object; but less abstractly and somewhat more concretely, physics is the interaction of a physical system of observation with a physical system being observed. Now, of course, physics still remains abstract, in that it deals with a certain aspect of reality or a certain ontic region (focusing on that aspect or region while abstracting from the others, that is, from the purely mathematical, the biological in the sense of the world in which we live, and the distinctively human historical realm). Nonetheless, the movement from classical physics to modern physics bears a thought-provoking resemblance to the movement from, say, Cartesian thought to Hegelian.

As we shall soon see in chapter 2, Kojève would soon find that Hegel had developed the final and definitive philosophy (of the human, historical world). But whereas Hegel had completed his philosophy of the human with a philosophy of nature that had the same dialectical character, Kojève considers that part of Hegelian philosophy to be false. For Kojève, classical physics was a decisive advance on earlier competing physical theories, and as we have seen, modern physics is a necessary advance over classical physics. It is worth noting that his position on (modern) physics and on (Hegelian) philosophy are very different. Regarding philosophy, he will argue that, at least in the decisive respect, Hegelian philosophy is true and definitive. Regarding physics, on the other hand, although he is certain that quantum physics represents an advance in the understanding of the basic objective reality of physical objects, he does not profess in any way to know that this state of knowledge is definitive. He believes it to be a step forward, but he is aware that certain important problems remain to be worked out; he expects that quantum physics will prevail and advance further, but he by no means excludes the possibility that it will in fact be replaced by a superior approach at some indefinite time in the future. The contrast is striking and puzzling: the philosophical evolution of mankind, he will soon assert, has come to a kind of completion; but the development by human beings of physics seems to be something that can continue indefinitely into the future.

What is the importance of this work for Kojève's development as a thinker? Certainly it is a necessary part of his ultimate project, uncompleted, of developing a complete philosophical system (or rather, as he came to envision it later, an updating of the Hegelian system of knowledge). The adequate philosopher must take account, and give an account, of physics. Furthermore, this development by Kojève of his knowledge of physics was crucial for his own thinking through of the project of updating Hegel's system, precisely on account of the inadequacy and unacceptability of Hegel's natural science. At the same time, Kojève's real knowledge of physics left him immune to the claims of social sciences to understand human affairs through the method of the natural sciences. All these themes will figure importantly in Kojève's work on the *System of Knowledge* in the 1950s; but for now, I must examine his most famous period of intellectual activity, his six-year endeavor to interpret Hegel's *Phenomenology of Spirit*.

NOTES

1. In *Revue d'histoire et de philosophie religieuses* 14 (1934): 534–554, and 15 (1935): 110–152.

2. Translated by Nina Ivanoff, edited by Laurent Bibard. Paris: Éditions Gallimard, 1998.

3. See Dominique Auffret's biography, *Alexandre Kojève: La philosophie, l'Etat, la fin de l'Histoire* (Paris: Editions Grasset & Fasquelle, 1990), 87–109, and his "Présentation" of the text of Kojève's *Idée du déterminisme dans la physique classique et dans la physique moderne*.

4. *Radicitus* ("by the roots" or "radically"): Lucretius, *De rerum natura* Book 3, line 877, in reference to the belief that there remains something of the soul after death.

5. *Introduction to the Reading of Hegel*, 187.

6. I heard Professor Henri Birault use, in a course on Nietzsche at the Sorbonne in 1969–1970, a phrase that I have always found especially helpful in thinking about this aspect of things: "La puissance possible de la pensée d'une possibilité" ("the possible power of the thought of a possibility").

7. *Introduction à la Lecture de Hegel*, 332 (a section not in the English translation).

8. "L'origine chrétienne de la science moderne" [The Christian origin of modern science], *Mélanges Alexandre Koyré*, volume 2 (Paris, 1964). English translation in *St. John's Review* 35, no. 1 (Winter 1984): 22–26.

Chapter Two

The Seminar on Hegel: History, Dialectic, and Finitude

Kojève's friend Alexandre Koyré taught a course on Hegel's religious philosophy at the École Pratique des Hautes Études in Paris during the year 1932–1933; having accepted a professorship in Cairo, he invited Kojève to continue the course. This led to a seminar that eventually lasted from 1933 to 1939, which Kojève devoted to understanding Hegel's *Phenomenology of Spirit*.

Several persons who attended the seminar have depicted Kojève's powerful impact. In his *Mémoires* Raymond Aron reports that during the seminar's final year he became a regular member "of the group of auditors that included Raymond Queneau, Jacques Lacan, Maurice Merleau-Ponty, Eric Weil, and Georges Fessard." He describes a typical session in these words:

> Kojève began by translating a few lines of the *Phenomenology*, heavily emphasizing certain words; then he spoke, without notes, never stumbling over a word, in an impeccable French to which his Slavic accent added a certain originality and charm. He fascinated an audience of superintellectuals inclined toward doubt or criticism. Why? His talent, his dialectical virtuosity had something to do with it. I do not know whether the speaker's art remains intact in the book that records the last year of the course, but that art, which had nothing to do with eloquence, was intimately connected with his subject and his personality. The subject was both world history and the *Phenomenology*. The latter shed light on the former. Everything took on meaning. Even those who were suspicious of historical providence, who suspected the artifice behind the art, did not resist the magician; at the moment, the intelligibility he conferred on the time and on events was enough of a proof. (Aron 1990, 65–66)

Georges Bataille described the impact on him of Kojève's classes as leaving him "broken, pulverized, killed ten times over: suffocated and immobilized [*cloué*, literally 'nailed down']" (Auffret 1990, 253).

Kojève's influence on French intellectual life, above all through this seminar, has been widely noted. Vincent Descombes labels one whole generation of French intellectual life the "generation of the three H's," that is, Hegel, Husserl, and Heidegger. He attributes the "triumphal return of Hegel" to prominence in French thinking to two things: the renewed interest in Marxism consequent upon the Russian Revolution, and "the influence of the course given by Alexandre Kojève at the Ecole Pratique des Hautes Études" (Descombes 1980, 9–10). Aimé Patri described Kojève in 1961 as "the unknown Superior whose dogma is revered, often unawares, by that important subdivision of the 'animal kingdom of the spirit' in the contemporary world—the progressivist intellectuals." He notes that the dissemination of Kojève's views through his seminar was "prior to the philosophico-political speculations of J. P. Sartre and M. Merleau-Ponty, to the publication of *les Temps Modernes* and the new orientation of *Esprit*, reviews which were the most important vehicles for the dissemination of progressivist ideology in France after the liberation." And he characterizes Kojève's influence in these terms:

> From that time we have breathed Kojève's teaching with the air of the times. . . . M. Kojève is, so far as we know, the first . . . to have attempted to constitute the intellectual and moral *ménage à trois* of Hegel, Marx and Heidegger which has since that time been such a great success. (Patri 1961, 234; quoted in editor's introduction to *Introduction to the Reading of Hegel*, vii)

After the war Raymond Queneau took the initiative of producing Kojève's book *Introduction à la Lecture de Hegel* on the basis of the lectures he presented to this famous seminar. (Kojève himself reviewed the whole text and added footnotes.) For the first years of the seminar, the book's content is based on notes taken during the seminar (as well as brief summaries of each year's proceedings taken from the annual publication of the École Pratique des Hautes Études). For the next to last year (1937–1938), the first six lectures are given in full from a stenographic record, and for the last year, 1938–1939, all twelve lectures are presented in full. Two appendices contain full texts of lectures from earlier years: appendix one, "The Dialectic of the Real and the Phenomenological Method in Hegel" presents the sixth through ninth lectures of 1934–1935, and appendix two, "The Idea of Death in the Philosophy of Hegel" presents the two last lectures from 1933–1934. Appendix three presents Kojève's analytical outline of Hegel's whole *Phenomenology of Spirit*.

The best-known aspect of Kojève's Hegelianism, apart from his claim about the end of history, is his analysis of the Master-Slave dialectic and his application of it as the underlying motive force of world history. Indeed, Kojève published his translation and line-by-line analysis of the relevant section of Hegel's *Phenomenology of Spirit* (section A of chapter IV) as an article entitled "Autonomy and Dependence of Self-Consciousness: Mastery and Slavery" in the journal *Mesures* in January 1939. This article is the only part of Kojève's interpretation of Hegel's *Phenomenology* published before the war and of whose publication Kojève himself took charge. He references this article for the basic understanding of Hegel on which he relies in two book manuscripts that he wrote during the war (on authority and on right, discussed in chapter 3 below). When the novelist Raymond Queneau undertook the task of putting together a book based on Kojève's seminar, he used this article from *Mesure* with the title "En Guise d'Introduction" (by way or in place of an introduction), as the book's first section.

In Hegel's *Phenomenology* the briefly presented master-slave dialectic appears to play a relatively small role in a large and complex book. Kojève famously or notoriously made it the key to the whole system, as the basic account of the first emergence of the human from the animal and of the motive force underlying subsequent human history. Or in other words, Kojève took the dialectic of master and slave to be the foundation and the vital core of Hegel's phenomenological anthropology.

Before turning to examine Kojève's interpretations of Hegel's text, I think a word is appropriate concerning the sense in which Kojève is and is not an interpreter of Hegel. A letter by Kojève himself to Tran-Duc-Thao is worth quoting at some length; it states Kojève's intention in regard to Hegel with clarity and in a way that I think any fair-minded reading of *Introduction à la Lecture de Hegel* fully confirms.

> My work did not have the character of an historical study; it was relatively unimportant for me to know what Hegel meant to say in his book; I conducted a course in phenomenological anthropology by putting Hegelian texts to use, but saying only what I considered to be the truth and letting drop what seemed to me to be an error in Hegel. Thus, in renouncing Hegelian monism, I consciously parted ways with that great philosopher. (In Jarczyk and Labarrière, 64)

He goes on to indicate as well that he consciously reinforced the role of the dialectic of master and slave. In short, Kojève follows Hegel because of his view that that great philosopher made the crucial final fundamental discoveries in philosophy; but Kojève seeks to develop the truest possible philosophical account and, if he finds something unsatisfactory in Hegel, he develops the argument differently.

Kojève's argument, conveyed as his introduction to and detailed commentary on Hegel's passage on mastery and slavery, sets forth from the observation that human beings are distinguished from other animals by being conscious of themselves, of their human reality and dignity. Such an observation certainly bears a resemblance either to the classic position that man is the rational animal together with Socrates' claim to be concerned above all with self-knowledge, or to the Cartesian definition of the human self as a thinking thing. Kojève critiques those older formulations for not adequately describing and *explaining* the human being. If man is a thinking thing, how did he become thus different from the other animals? The theoretical or contemplative thinker loses himself in, is absorbed by, the object of his thought. But what does a thinking thing know about itself? How can it come to take a distance on itself so as to be able to make itself an object of its contemplative thought? Can it give a coherent account of itself as a thinking being, explaining how it knows what it knows, including what it knows about itself?

Kojève points out that the contemplative thinker, absorbed in the object of thought, is brought back to himself by desire, which makes one aware of oneself as a desiring being, and which tends to motivate one to action that aims at satisfying desire. The self, in fact, is most deeply constituted by the character of its desire (and of its consequent actions and satisfactions). Purely animal, biological desires, ultimately connected with the biological goals of self-preservation and procreation, constitute a purely animal self—one, in Kojève's analysis, that attains the level of sentiment or feeling of self but not self-consciousness. Desire is not a given being like other real objects, but the presence of an absence; animal desire aims directly at a natural object and fills itself with that natural content. If the human is to differ from the natural animal reality, the human being must be characterized by a desire that is different from animal desire and that has a different object from the things that are objects of animal desire. Now, desire itself is such an object that differs from things to which natural desire is directed; desire is an emptiness, a nothingness, the presence of an absence. Distinctively human desire is the desire not of some natural good things but of desire itself; that is, it is the desire to put oneself in the place of the object of the other's desire, to be oneself the object of desire, or to be recognized as an autonomous value or as having intrinsic dignity. This is Kojève's way of discovering and elaborating what Hegel calls the desire for recognition (and which Kojève also calls a desire for pure prestige).[1]

Now, for this distinctively human being to exist in reality, the distinctively human desire must win out over all the natural animal desires (which themselves are all subordinated to or constituent elements of the desire to preserve life). This can come to pass if and only if the distinctively human desire in question prevails over the totality of the biological or vitalistic desires, that is, if the desire in question leads the human to act in accordance with that desire over all the self-preserving desires, or in other words to risk his life for the sake of recognition (the object of the distinctively human desire). The initial anthropogenetic situation must, therefore, be social: it involves two or more persons, not one only. Both must be moved by the distinctively human urge for recognition, that is, by the desire to make the other respect his worth and dignity; to do this, both are willing to risk their lives, and so they approach each other with hostile intent willing to go the distance in risking their lives. For a human reality (that is, human being as actually and verifiably existing in external reality) to come into being, then, it will have to be as a recognized human reality, that is, a human being recognized by another (or others) in his distinctively human dignity. If both proto-humans persevere to the end in their fight for recognition, one or both will be dead and no real recognition will come to pass. For actual recognition to come into being, both combatants must remain alive. The way this can happen, in turn, is that one man, faced with the imminent danger of death, by an act of freedom chooses to give up the fight, to recognize the other as master and to accept his own status as slave rather than to persevere to the death in the fight for recognition.

At first sight, accordingly, the master appears to be the only fully human person. He has realized his humanity through persevering to the end in the fight for recognition and has achieved the recognition (by the slave) that he sought. The real social situation thus created supports the humanity of the master, his freedom (from being determined by merely biological, animal, vital motives), and of course his superiority. He likewise attains leisure, since he forces the slave to work for him. Hence he attains freedom in relation to the natural world in another way too: instead of having to work for the satisfaction of his natural desires, he can satisfy them through the work of the slave. But in fact his situation is, in Kojève's striking phrase, "une impasse existentielle," an existential dead end. The whole purpose of risking his life was to win recognition (of his distinctively human value and dignity). But recognition, to be satisfying, has to come from someone whom one respects, whom one recognizes reciprocally or mutually. The master, however, precisely cannot extend recognition to the slave, who has refused to go all the way in the risk of life and who has plainly accepted a position of inferiority to the master; accordingly, the master's risk has been in fact for the sake of something without real value for him. And looking around him in the world, the master sees no other status to which he could aspire.

On the side of the slave, of course, everything is different. The slave in choosing to refuse the risk of life has not yet realized his humanity as the master has; he has chosen slavery with security instead of free mastery won through risk, and in that way appears to have bound himself to dependency upon the natural biological given world (from which the master has achieved a certain freedom). But the slave's situation does have distinctively human elements in it: awareness of death and finitude, forced work, and the capacity to aspire to an ideal. The slave gave up the fight for recognition through an awareness of impending death, of the loss of everything valuable; his whole being was shaken by the prospect of death, and so he gained an insight into the essential mortality and finitude of human being. By surrendering, he clung to that finite life on the condition of working for the master. Work, as distinguished from the animal's immediate pursuit of the object of desire, actualizes (at first sight paradoxically) a kind of freedom from nature. One makes something of value which one does not immediately consume; one thus takes a distance on it and can think about its varied uses and possibilities, including the possibility of exchanging it for something else. Forced to work without that work's being tied to immediate satisfaction of desire, the slave also discovers the freedom to devise new ways of performing his tasks, of producing things, of inventing new things. And so the whole distinctively human side of creating a human world (artisanal and eventually technological) within and against the natural world emerges on the slaves' side of the human, social world. Finally, whereas the master could never be satisfied with the recognition conferred on him by slaves, let alone wish to become slave himself, the slave, deprived of freedom, has before his eyes the ideal of freedom in the person of the master. The slave needs only to bring it about that he wins freedom and recognition from the master (who thus becomes a former master) in order to achieve a definitive satisfaction of the desire for recognition. And so the future of historical development lies on the side of the slaves.

To be completed in the fullness of time, historical progress will ultimately require (among other things) a violent revolution whereby the slaves take up the struggle with risk of life that at the origin of history they refused. The path of this history, of course, is long and complex: the transformation of the original Greek world of pagan masters through Alexander the Great's universal empire; the destruction of that world through the Roman Empire; its transformation through the Christian religion; the eventual secularization and hence realization in this world of Christian ideas in the history of modern Europe, culminating in Napoleon's universal dissemination and (in principle) establishment of the rights of man; and so on. This account has a decidedly Marxist flavor to it in the emphasis upon the workers as the active agents of historical advance, and Kojève even appears to take the Soviet revolution as the final type of revolution that will establish universal recognition of each by all. Indeed, he signals the Marxist character of his Hegelianism through an epigraph of Marx that attributes to Hegel the primacy of work in the life of mankind: "Hegel . . . erfasst die *Arbeit* als das *Wesen*, als das sich bewährende Wesen des Menschen" ("Hegel . . . posits *work* as the *essence*, as the self-verifying essence, of man"). At the same time, Kojève's analysis of the necessity of the master's role at the beginning of human history and of the necessary place of the fight or struggle with real risk of life insists on this other dimension of human negativity which, in his view, Marx wrongly deemphasized.

The key feature of human being in the world (since one cannot properly say human nature, given that the distinctively human was freely created by proto-humans in a rejection, a negation, of the natural) is that the human being is not defined by its nature, nor by its place in the natural world, nor simply by what it is. On the contrary, the human being comes into being through negativity, that is, through a negation or rejection of that natural order, including what it itself was by nature. The human being is not simply what it is, but becomes what it will be. The specifically human reality arises through the freely chosen risk of life, which amounts to a rejection of the most powerful natural impulses, a negation of the defining limits of nature. That human origin creates an awareness of the nothingness of human being, its essential negativity, its finitude. The kinds of human activity and the character of human awareness are affected by that original human insight into mortality (however much, in the course of history, human beings create beliefs that tend to hide their mortality from themselves, most notably through beliefs in an unending afterlife).

This fundamental anthropology reminds one of the Heideggerian living toward death; indeed several critics (including A. Patri, cited earlier) have accused Kojève of following Heidegger rather more than Hegel in his interpretation of man and history. Kojève certainly acknowledges his indebtedness to Heidegger's phenomenological anthropology in several places. In a footnote to *Introduction to the Reading of Hegel*, he offers the opinion that Heidegger's *Sein und Zeit* is "without a doubt remarkable and authentically philosophical." He writes that it "adds, fundamentally, nothing new to the anthropology of the *Phenomenology*," but Hegel's work in Kojève's judgment "would probably never have been understood if Heidegger had not published his book" (*Introduction to the Reading of Hegel*, 259). Some ten years later, in the preface to his attempt to update the Hegelian system (written in the mid-fifties), he again stated that Heidegger played a crucial role in his own understanding. The guidance of Koyré and Kojève's own vast and encyclopedic learning were necessary and helpful but not by themselves sufficient to enable him to understand Hegel:

> But this would not have sufficed if I had not read Heidegger's *Sein und Zeit*. I therefore consider that it is my duty in this place to mention the name of that philosopher of genius, who, by the way, has taken a bad turn philosophically, perhaps precisely because of an unfortunate desire to "surpass" Hegel by "returning to" . . . Plato at first (via Husserl), next to Aristotle, then to . . . Hölderlin and finally to Parmenides, or rather to Heraclitus, or again to whomever. (*Le Concept, le Temps et le Discours*, 32–33)

Human being as partaking most distinctively of negativity is the fundamental basis of a number of human phenomena: most importantly, freedom. Kojève finds it necessary to understand freedom in a very strong sense, which manifests itself in reality not just by the ability to choose between two or more alternatives that are naturally present (which other animals certainly appear to do) but by the capacity to make things altogether new, to change things fundamentally or radically, to create what has not hitherto existed. The human being is not defined by, that is to say limited by, nature. Through negativity he can reject anything in nature. Some rejections will produce madness, illusion, failure; in pursuing some, the man will fail and, together with the failed illusions, he will be annihilated. But other rejections of the natural given will produce ideals that men succeed in imposing upon the real natural and the really given human/social worlds. And so, in place of a life according to nature in a naturally defined place in the natural cosmos, human beings create a technological world that must exist within nature but that also stands against and gives them power over nature (first explicitly formulated as a goal in the modern Baconian-Cartesian project of the conquest of nature). And in the human/social world, men are not bound to naturally originating orders, castes, and institutions; they can create new modes of social and political organization, culminating in the universal and homogeneous state as the ultimate product of human rationality.

In this first introduction to his interpretation of Hegel, then, we already see that Kojève's Hegelianism partakes of aspects of Marx and Heidegger. What are the fundamental claims and main traits of his Hegelianism as he developed it further? I think I can formulate the best brief answer to this question by discussing the first appendix of the *Introduction to the Reading of Hegel*, called "The Dialectic of the Real and the Phenomenological Method in Hegel." This section, the complete text of four lectures from Kojève's course of the year 1934–1935, seeks to clarify the dialectical character of Hegel's system. All philosophers' thinking and teaching, at least since Socrates, have been dialectical, whether in the Socratic manner as the refutative testing of beliefs, opinions, and other assertions against their opposites, or in the manner of later philosophers who engaged in dialectical exchanges with preceding schools of philosophical thought. As Kojève expounds it, Hegel's system is dialectical in a different way, and not because of the specific character of the thinker's activity. The Hegelian method is one of pure phenomenological description of concrete realities. The Hegelian system is dialectical because the reality that it describes is dialectical: that is, the beings described—for simplicity let's just say for now, in this context, human beings—are themselves dialectical. That is, human beings are not simply given beings that remain eternally identical to themselves, but are a threefold identity, negativity, and totality, which is in turn a new identity (or the more familiar thesis, antithesis, and synthesis, which is in turn a new thesis). The being in its identity can and does negate something about that identity and so becomes in part opposite; yet it maintains a continuity of being, preserving something of its original identity (for example, through remembering) so that it ends up a new totality that preserves something of the original identity together with its negation. This negativity is the key to radical freedom, through which a human being is not determined once and for all in all decisive respects by what is given in its initial being, whether what is fundamentally given about that being is given by nature, by society, by culture, or by anything else.

For human beings, manifestations of negativity typically involve thought: conceptions of what the world is, what man is, how one should live, how men do or ought to relate to each other, what justice is, and so on. Kojève subscribes to a realistic definition of truth: truth is reality revealed in coherent speech, or speech that adequately reveals a reality, or the adequation of speech with reality. Now, when a human being gives verbal expression to the negativity that is fundamental to specifically human being, he is doing something other than simply stating a phenomenological description of what is. Through negativity, he is rejecting what really exists (or some aspect of it) and instead speaking of something that does not really exist (at all, or in some relevant aspect); in consequence, such speech is rather error than truth, since there is not—or perhaps not yet—an adequate correspondence of such speech to concrete reality. The Hegelian dialectical conception of Being makes possible a full understanding of error, and the deep sense of *errare humanum est* ("to err is human" or, one could say, "the human is to err"). Only human beings can err, can live in error, and can keep error alive (possibly later to become truth), whereas Nature eliminates its errors (for example, defectively formed animals). And given the element of negativity in being, we can on that basis understand, or speak coherently about, fundamental change in human history—change such that what once was error may, through subsequent actions that negate given being, become truth. What I have here called errors include illusions, delusions, ideas, ideals, religious beliefs, and projects for the future (these latter would not in normal usage be called errors, even though they certainly cannot yet be called truths, when the projector is fully aware that he is aiming at something that does not yet exist).

When we seek the truth, including the truth about ourselves, as seekers of truth we experience the need to understand how we can know what we know. If all our speeches (definitions, coherent assertions, arguments) must always change with the flux of time (because all the beings that exist in the flux of time are subject to constant change), these speeches cannot reveal truths in any sense worthy of the name. Any assertion could reasonably be contradicted the very next moment; and if that is the case, one's speech does not really assert anything that endures in time. Each speech one may make is contradicted by its opposite, which has no less claim to truth; and so the totality of one's discourse is in a decisive respect no different from silence. Such speeches could only amount to what Kojève calls "le bavardage infini" or "indéfini," unending or indefinite chatter. Earlier philosophic positions sought to establish truth in a strong sense through some relation to what is eternal, but ran aground on making sense of how we can have access to such eternal grounds of truth while we are at the same time beings living in the flux of the spatial-temporal world, free, and subject to error. Only on the basis of Hegelian dialectic can one give a full account of how the knower comes to know things, including the full understanding of himself as knower: contemplating the historical development of beings, one can see how human negativity produces change and transforms former errors into truths; the philosopher looking back at these developments can grasp how man became what he is and made into truths various earlier expressions of his free or creative negativity (errors, crimes, ideals). Retrospectively—and only retrospectively—one can understand the rational necessity of the totality of those developments; thus one can eventually understand the truth, including how one comes to understand the truth, because one grasps that that truth is in fact the outcome of one's own doing or making. Truth then is always retrospective, after the fact, *a posteriori*, as is implicit for Kojève in a passage from the article "Hegel, Marx, and Christianity" that I quote at length in chapter 4, or as evidently applies to Hegel from the famous phrase in the preface to his *Philosophy of Right*: "The owl of Minerva begins its flight only at dusk."

Human being, then, is radically free. The human being is not a given nature, fixed once and for all in or by nature; nor is it a merely natural being that happens to have otherwise undetermined choices among alternative natural goods. Rather, the human being is something that creates itself (thanks to Being's aspect of negativity) in time. If this is true, one of two things follows. Either the human being is forever indeterminate or open-ended, in which case no truth in the strong sense, no genuine rational (coherent discursive) knowledge, is possible. Or the number of possible modes of human being (and therefore knowing) is finite, and historical development can come to some kind of completion or end, so that retrospective knowledge can be definitive, not ready to change again (that is to say, to be falsified) with time. Kojève, of course, is best known for his argument that there must be an end of history. This baffling assertion that history has attained its end or fulfillment, as I have noted before, is what most people are likely to think of upon hearing the name Alexandre Kojève, if they think of anything at all, especially since the remarkable popularization of that thesis through Francis Fukuyama's article and book some dozen years ago.

Having completed this brief discussion of the fundamental character of Kojève's Hegelianism, I turn now to investigate further his notorious claim about the end of history. What are his observations and arguments in support of the notion of an end of history? In the *Introduction to the Reading of Hegel*, he deals with this especially, as one would expect, in the last year of the course, 1938–1939, devoted to the interpretation of chapter 8 of the *Phenomenology of Spirit*, entitled "Das absolute Wissen" ("Absolute Knowledge"). (It is our good fortune that a complete transcript of the last year of the course was preserved and published in the book.) The first two lectures for that year are grouped together under the title "Philosophy and Wisdom." Exploring the notions of the philosopher and of the wise man, Kojève investigates the meaning of Hegel's claim to have attained "Absolute Knowledge." Regarding the premises of this whole development, Kojève adds to Hegel's analysis—or makes explicit something only implicit in Hegel's account—by specifying that not only must one posit, as Hegel did, that man is self-consciousness, but one must posit the existence of a self-consciousness that seeks to expand itself as far as possible, to explore any new realities, and to discover, articulate, and seek to resolve contradictions. In other words, one must posit the existence among human beings of the philosopher. Otherwise, one could in principle imagine that mankind might get stuck forever at some incomplete stage of human history. The philosopher's articulate awareness is a necessary presupposition, in Kojève's account of the matter, if humanity is to be sure to move beyond any given incomplete historical era.

In this manner, then, Kojève attributes to philosophers a crucial role in historical progress. He appears to assign to the philosopher an activist role beyond merely coming to full consciousness of a historical era that has been completely developed.[2] Thus he seems to take a position that is more intellectualist (or idealist) and activist (as regards the role of the philosopher) than Hegel's, let alone Marx's. Hegel, after all, described philosophers as understanding a historical form of world Spirit only when it was completed, and Marx distinguished his goal of scientific socialism, as something that must necessarily arise as the next step in historical development, from the mere ideals of utopian socialism. In fact, Kojève explores the possible role of philosophers as activists in the historical process further and develops it in more detail, although with considerable complexity and qualifications, in his later critique of Leo Strauss. Thus, on the one hand, he seems more idealist than Marx. But on the other hand, he seems Marxist rather than Hegelian in seeing the end of history as lying still in the future, rather as Marx himself, although characterizing himself as materialist, described the leading edge of intellectuals as going over as activists to the progressive side of the final revolutionary class—and exhorted them to do so. (For this reason, among others,

Kojève rejects Marx's self-description as materialist and likewise declines to accept that Marx believed in the possibility that anything future can be determined and known in advance rather than being a matter of contingency. One may infer that Kojève took certain actual statements by Marx about the necessity of the communist revolution to be political rhetoric or propaganda rather than philosophical assertion. Still less does Kojève accept the dogmatic materialism of various Marxist intellectuals who were his contemporaries.)

Kojève argues that Hegel's great discovery is the criterion of circularity to establish the truth of a coherent discourse; that in starting a process of questioning (toward full self-knowledge), one will develop a series of questions and answers that eventually leads one back around to one's starting point. Or in other words, the coherent discourse will show itself to have passed through and so to comprehend all possible alternatives. This circularity, rather than a relation to something eternal, according to Kojève, is Hegel's newly discovered criterion of comprehensive truth. And Hegel can expound a circular coherent discourse because reality, the development of human history, has itself completed a development that is in an essential respect circular, in that it has completed the circle of possible alternatives, ending in a position that can be discursively shown to be satisfactory.

When he examines Hegel's claim about history's fulfillment, however, Kojève finds that, on the level of historical phenomena, history does not in fact seem to have been completed. We do not have the Universal and Homogeneous State, with the full recognition of each individual's dignity through the universal. He argued, as he would still reiterate in 1946, that Hegel's teaching is therefore not a truth in the full sense, since his discourse does not correspond to an objective reality (or reality does not yet correspond to his discourse); but the teaching is not simply false, not simply an error, either, because one cannot show that the Universal and Homogeneous State is impossible. Neither truth nor falsehood simply, it can be taken as an ideal, a project, that further human historical action may transform into truth. Philosophically guided political action could thus produce the truth of Hegel's discourse by completing the transformation of worldly reality in accord with the Hegelian understanding. We can thus see here more clearly how crucially important, according to Kojève, philosophers are for the world's historical development.

Kojève elaborated the philosophers' effect on history in substantially more detail in his essay published in *Critique* in 1950, "L'Action Politique des Philosophes" ("The Political Action of Philosophers"), which presented an extensive criticism of Leo Strauss's interpretation of Xenophon's dialogue *On Tyranny*. (The essay's title was changed to the more provocative "Tyranny and Wisdom" when it was republished in the book *De la Tyrannie*, which also contained Strauss's work on Xenophon as well as his response to Kojève.) Kojève argues that there has always been an unresolved problem regarding the possibility of a philosopher's acting in politics. On the one hand, the philosopher by definition, and in reality, has a single-minded devotion to the pursuit of wisdom and the acquisition of knowledge. On the other hand, effective action in politics requires detailed concrete knowledge of all the relevant particulars of any given political order and situation, and the acquisition of this kind of knowledge and its application is also a full-time job. The philosopher needs to be concerned with his effect on society, because he needs to test his ideas through confronting other people in society with them (he cannot rest satisfied with mere subjective certainty, which might be mad or otherwise illusory). Furthermore, he would wish to draw others to his way of thinking, perhaps most notably by seeking to educate other people in society in his ideas. Thus he is brought toward necessarily interacting with society and hence toward having political concerns. But to be effective in pursuing those political concerns would involve compromising, if only through loss of time, his philosophical enterprise. Kojève claims that no political philosopher has convincingly presented any discursive resolution to this problem. He argues in a Hegelian manner, however, that this problem has in fact been solved by history. Philosophers have had a powerful effect on history. Alexander the Great applied in reality certain ideas of Greek, and particularly Aristotelian, philosophy, in creating the first universal empire; he put into political practice the philosophical idea of mankind as universal, comprehending Athenian and Spartan and Macedonian, Greek and barbarian. Rejecting the political relevance of ethnicity and heredity, he acted toward a universal empire, and promoted that goal in practice through the biological means of encouraging intermarriage between his Macedonian conquerors and the various conquered peoples. The philosophical founders of the Enlightenment were not themselves political revolutionaries, but their intellectual descendants (the *philosophes*) did eventually influence political actors to such an extent as to bring about the French Revolution and the practical political spread of its ideas and practices through Napoleon. Most recently, Kojève argues, we have seen a philosopher's (Hegel's) ideas adapted to be more accessible to political actors by the intellectual (Marx), and then put into practice by the tyrant (Lenin, Stalin). Thus, shortly after World War II, Kojève, in debate with Strauss, continued to assert the philosopher's effect on political action (through the mediation, he makes clear now, of intellectuals).

Returning to the final year of his seminar, we see that in his stance toward the end of history, Kojève at this point resembles Marx; with the important difference already noted, however, that whereas Marx (at least much of the time, if not always) held that "scientific" as opposed to "utopian" socialism spoke of what must necessarily take place, Kojève emphasizes here and everywhere that history as the development of Spirit has the form of a free contingent process (*in der Form des freien zufälligen Geschehens*) (*Introduction to the Reading of Hegel*, 152, quoting from chapter 8 of Hegel's *Phenomenology*) and can therefore be truly understood only after the fact.

But regarding this issue of whether an end to history has come and whether the perfect state exists, as Kojève says, "what is involved is a verification of *fact*, that is to say, of something essentially *uncertain*" (*Introduction to the Reading of Hegel*, 98). More important is to see whether the discursive system of wisdom itself that Hegel presented is circular. This means that one must not only verify that the *Phenomenology of Spirit* is circular, but that the *Logic* or *Encyclopaedia* is also circular, and furthermore that the philosophic system of Hegel taken as a whole (*Phenomenology* and *Encyclopedia* together) constitutes a circular system. Now, on this latter question, Kojève says, "It is precisely there that the non-circularity of Hegel's system is perfectly obvious" (*Introduction to the Reading of Hegel*, 98n9). In other words, if Hegel thought he had fully completed philosophy and attained wisdom or absolute knowledge, he was mistaken. I take it that, in saying this about Hegel's system, Kojève was referring above all to what was clearly his most fundamental and far-reaching disagreement with Hegel, namely his view that the Hegelian philosophy of nature, meant to be the discursive account of the whole in which man arises, is erroneous and thus leaves the system incomplete. Kojève of course was a serious student of physics, as we have seen, and on that basis he held that contemporary physics was in fact successfully developing valid and necessary knowledge in its distinctive manner. As compared to genuine physical science, he called Hegel's science of nature "magical," and dismissed Hegel's attack on Newton as "insensate" (*Introduction to the Reading of Hegel*, 146).

Now this difference between Kojève and Hegel is no small matter; it involves not only the question of the proper character of physics and its place in or relation to comprehensive philosophical discourse, but also the most fundamental question of ontology. In Kojève's view, Hegel's great discovery on the level of ontology was the development of the dialectical ontology of identity, negativity, and totality. Discovering this new ontology, however, Hegel clung to the monist philosophical tradition and therefore extended his dialectical ontology to all of being. Since this approach fails in its application to nature, however, Kojève rejects it and keeps the Hegelian ontology only for the human/historical realm and holds that a different ontology must apply to the realm of nature. Accordingly, it seems that considerable additional philosophical work is needed truly to complete the Hegelian system. In the *Introduction to the Reading of Hegel*, Kojève barely suggests the main lines of such a future development. In a footnote toward the end of his three-lecture treatment in the last year of the course entitled "A Note on Eternity, Time, and the Concept," he suggests that the remedy for the inadequacies of Hegel's system (which stem from his monism, that is, the inappropriate application of the dialectical analysis of being to nature as well as to the human world) might be "to combine Plato's conception (for the mathematical, or better, geometrical substructure of the World) with Aristotle's (for its biological structure) and Kant's (for its physical, or better, dynamic, structure), while reserving Hegelian dialect for Man and History" (*Introduction to the Reading of Hegel*, 147n36). To work out such a philosophical project, surely, would be no small task. Kojève's later philosophical writings of the fifties, which set forth on the project of updating the complete Hegelian system, can be understood as preparing to deal with the working out of these problems.

The sixth through eighth lectures of 1938–1939, "A Note on Eternity, Time, and the Concept," state Kojève's key insight into Hegel's culminating position in the history of philosophy. The importance of this account for Kojève's own thinking finds expression in the fact that he was to restate the account both more briefly and at very much greater length in the 1950s—more briefly in an article "Le Concept et le Temps" ("Time and the Concept"), published in an issue of *Deucalion* devoted to Hegel; at much greater length in his own volumes that introduce the project of updating Hegel's system of knowledge (discussed below in chapter 5). "A Note on Eternity, Time, and the Concept" presents a schematized history of philosophy that seeks to show that philosophy has evolved in a way that exhausts all possibilities and so has come to its conclusion.

Here are the bare bones of the argument. By "the Concept" Kojève means the totality of coherent (noncontradictory) discourse that a philosopher articulates in the attempt to answer the important questions about himself and the world while giving an account of how such philosophical understanding is possible. The Concept takes time to develop and appears in time; it is not itself temporal, however. If the Concept were temporal, that would mean that when one asserts something as true, one might well assert the opposite the next moment, and so one would end up asserting precisely nothing; in that case there is no philosophical Concept, but only what Kojève later calls "unending chatter." He rejects this possibility as philosophically without interest; what I find to be his most powerful statement of that rejection was formulated in his discussion of Kant in the 1955 article "Le Temps et Le Concept":

> The *temporal* so-called "concept," i.e. a concept by definition *variable* and thus multiple and varied, is in effect nothing but the aggregation of the "notions" with which men have peopled the world since they began to speak in it and

which allow them to fabricate the discourses that non-philosophers of all types make everywhere and since always in order to communicate mutually with each other, with a view to making them "recognize" the different "personal opinions" that they *have*, to be sure, and to which they *hold* with more or less *conviction*, *faith* or *force*, but of which it is absolutely impossible to say whether they are *true* or *false*, although one can draw conclusions about their "orthodoxy" or "heterodoxy" by establishing their "success" or their "failure" in the natural and historical *given* world in which they are emitted. (14)

The Concept, then, must be something other than "temporal," other than the Heraclitean "everything flows." Most opposite to this Heraclitean flux, of course, is the position developed by Parmenides (and in modern times, according to Kojève, by Spinoza): the Concept is Eternity itself. But then paradoxes ensue—most notably that if Eternity is the Concept, no change, time, difference, or anything else about which we speak can be part of it: the Concept could not be discourse or *logos*; it would be pure silence. Of Heraclitean discourse, nothing is true; of Parmenidean truth, nothing can be said.

Plato and Aristotle, therefore, have every motivation to try to find another way of grounding the possibility of philosophical truth. They hold that the Concept is eternal (not temporal) but not Eternity itself. Since the Concept exists in time (in the minds and speeches, for instance, of us who live and think in the temporal-spatial world), the Concept to be eternal is conceived as standing in some relation with Eternity. For Plato, the eternal Concept is related to an eternity or to eternal being or beings that stand outside time (the Platonic forms or ideas, and ultimately the One Good). For Aristotle, the eternal concept is related to an eternity or to eternal beings that exist in time, like fixed patterns, eddies, within the stream of Heraclitean becoming (the permanent species of things). For both Plato and Aristotle, the inadequately answered questions involve how we can understand the access that we, who live in a temporal-spatial world of flux, can have to eternal concepts; how to explain human freedom if we in fact are thus linked with the eternal; and how to grasp the possibility and character of error.

For Kant as for the others, the Concept must be eternal; but now, seeking to avoid the problems of Parmenides and Spinoza on the one hand, Plato and Aristotle on the other, Kant relates the eternal concept not to Eternity but to time itself. Kant's argument is of course dense and complex, as all readers of the *Critique of Pure Reason* know only too well, but Kojève states the essential that is needed to fill out his schematization. Kant famously stated that "without the concept intuition is blind; and without intuition the concept is empty." Truth with substantive content must therefore involve intuitions (experience of the spatial-temporal world), and all these take place in time. The eternal concept relates to time as the ways (the twelve concepts-categories, all which according to Kant must be schematized or related to time) in which our minds, by transcendental necessity, must grasp our intuitions of temporal things in the world. The transcendental, in turn, means that which precedes temporal experience but which is necessary to make temporal experience such as we have it possible; it includes certain theoretical principles in accordance with which our intuitions necessarily take place, such as the law of causality. Human thinking takes time and must necessarily use concepts that are related to time; another kind of being (God, say) might be able to think about nontemporal being (e.g., the eternal whole of being), but we have no access in thought to such eternal being.

Hegel, finally, takes the last step that is possible in accordance with this schema: he asserts that the Concept (which for Hegel too is eternal in some sense, in that having once come into being as definitive knowledge, it will change no more) *is* time itself. He even (unlike the other philosophers with whom Kojève deals in these three lectures) states it in so many words in the *Phenomenology*, in fact twice: "'Was die *Zeit* betrifft . . . so is sie der daseiende Begriff selbst' ['As for Time . . . it is the empirically existing Concept itself']" (131–132). This assertion sounds baffling, and for Kojève it would be incomprehensible if by time what was meant was the time of modern physics; but time here means negativity; action that transforms the given reality; human, historical time. Conceptual understanding is possible, according to Kojève's Hegel, only by detaching the essential content from the real temporal existence of something which passes into nonbeing. Fond of the strikingly paradoxical formulation, Kojève quotes Hegel's saying from chapter 7 of the *Phenomenology* that "conceptual understanding is equivalent to a murder," and he comments in a footnote that it may be no accident that certain aspects of understanding (for instance, full understanding of the concept "dog") do in fact require the death of the object understood (in the dog's dissection). He clarifies the point in a footnote comparing Aristotle and Hegel:

> For Aristotle there is a concept "dog" only because there is an *eternal* real dog, namely, the *species* "dog," which is always in the present; for Hegel, on the other hand, there is a concept "dog" only because the real dog is a *temporal* entity — that is, an essentially finite or "mortal" entity, an entity which is annihilated at every instant: and the Concept *is* the permanent support of this nihilation of the spatial real, which nihilation is itself nothing other than *Time*. (141n32)

Hegel's approach, unlike Aristotle's, can explain the conceptual knowledge we have of extinct species (even in the absence of fossil remains). The Concept grasps conceptually what passes out of existence into the nonbeing of the past. Thus the Concept, becoming eternal at the end, is the product of a successive series of negations, differentiations, temporalizations; the Hegelian science is the synthetic integration of all the theses, antitheses, and partial syntheses that have taken place over time (historical time in which changes arising from negativity take place and relegate present realities to the unreality of the past), and in this sense the Concept *is* time.

In this context Kojève presents a helpful elaboration of the structure of human time in Hegel's account in a way that enables one to state clearly what constitutes a historically significant action. This Hegelian conception of time is also, in his view, necessary for giving a coherent account of the conception of man (originally a prephilosophic Judeo-Christian conception) as a free and historical individual and to understand humanity as creating itself in history. Physical or cosmic time is characterized by the primacy of the present. In fact, Kojève wonders whether such time really should be called time at all; modern physics, after all, treats time as a fourth spatial dimension and so may be said to try to represent all of objective reality simultaneously as present, without a truly temporal dimension (127n15).[3] Biological time is characterized by the primacy of the past. It is "Aristotle's circular time; it is *Eternity* in Time; it is Time in which everything changes in order to remain the same thing" (138n28). Historical or human time exhibits the primacy of the future and has "the rhythm Future → Past → Present." The distinctively human involves the (unreal) future's effective presence through desire and action, which, based on the actual past, negates the present to bring about something new. In sum, it seems "that the physical or cosmic object is but a simple *presence (Gegenwart)*, whereas the fundamental biological phenomenon is probably *Memory* in the broad sense, and the specifically human phenomenon is without a doubt the *Project*" (134n21).

Kojève elaborates the point by explaining what makes a moment "historical":

> We say that a moment is "historical" when the action that is performed in it is performed in terms of the idea that the agent has of the future (that is, in terms of a *Project*): one decides on a *future* war, and so on; therefore, one acts in terms of the *future*. But if the moment is to be truly "historical," there must be *change*; in other words, the decision must be *negative* with respect to the given: in deciding for the future war, one decides *against* the prevailing peace. And, through the decision for the future war, the peace is transformed into the past. Now, the *present* historical act, *launched* by the idea of the future (by the Project), is *determined* by this past that it creates: if the peace is sure and honorable, the negation that relegates it to the past is the act of a madman or a criminal; if it is humiliating, its negation is an act worthy of a stateman; and so on. (136n24)

A detailed discussion of the example of Caesar's walking at night along the banks of the Rubicon illustrates the point. What makes the moment historic is, of course, above all the project for the future that Caesar is contemplating: to invade Rome, to overthrow the existing republic, and so forth. But the genuinely historical moment must pass through the past: if some ordinary soldier were thinking about this, it would be daydream or madness; it is historic because of Caesar's past actions, which have established the real possibility of his proceeding with this project successfully. (It must be a real possibility but not a certainty; for certainty would imply that the moment was altogether determined by the past and so would not be a new project nor genuinely something future.) "Consequently, there is a 'historic moment' only when the *present* is ordered in terms of the *future*, on the condition that the future makes its way into the present not in an *immediate* manner (*unmittelbar*; the case of a utopia), but having been *mediated* (*vermittelt*) by the *past*—that is, by an *already accomplished* action" (137n25).

From Kojève's schematization of the history of philosophy, one can readily see a sense in which the development of philosophical thinking can be said to have completed a circle, to have exhausted all the possibilities, to have developed all the basic philosophical positions, which are finite in number. Thus, for Kojève, Hegel correctly sees that philosophical development has come to its completion. This claim, however, must be qualified or limited in the way that I have noted earlier. Hegel's monism is erroneous; his dialectical ontology applies to human being and history but not to the realm of Nature. Hence some final philosophical tidying up, at the very least, is needed: to show how the dialectical ontology of human things (exhibiting a time in which the future has primacy) can cohere with a different kind of ontology for physics (for which time is primarily the present) and biology (with a biological time in which the past has primacy). I imagine that most of us are inclined to suspect that such a task would, in fact, amount to a lot more than tying up loose ends; it might need to be quite a philosophical achievement in its own right (although, in Kojève's judgment, it would not be the discovery of something fundamentally new).

In the last lectures of the course, Kojève elaborates his interpretation of the Hegelian view of Spirit completing its development, a final reconciliation of Spirit and world, the coming into being of definitive systematic knowledge. In the very last lecture, Kojève wrestles with some puzzling points about the end of history. The full development of Spirit means the coming into existence of definitive knowledge. Spirit is neither subject nor object but the product of their interaction; that is, it is discursive thought revealing Being, or Being revealed by discursive thought. Throughout history thinking subjects have stood in opposition to objects thought. In fact thinking subject taken by itself and object thought taken by itself are both abstractions; what really exists is Spirit (objects revealed by thought and thought revealing objects). Concrete man,

Spirit, has throughout history been something that is coming into being as the product of the oppositions between subject (thinker and actor) and objects (world, other people, and self as object of thought). Now if truth is the adequation of coherent speech (and thought) to reality, the opposition between thinking and reality is rather error than truth, and as we have seen, man during history is characterized much more by error than by truth. But the end of history means the end of the opposition between man and world through the coming into being of adequate knowledge. Therefore a reconciliation of man, or a new harmony of man, with the world (including the then given social human world) emerges. Philosophy gives way to wisdom. Man in the historical sense disappears, but not in any natural or biological catastrophe. Rather, Man as action negating the given, as error, as philosopher rather than wise man, disappears. Kojève notes that Marx dealt with these themes:

> History properly so-called, in which men ("classes") fight among themselves for recognition and fight against Nature by work, is called in Marx "Realm of necessity" (*Reich der Notwendigkeit*); beyond (*jenseits*) is situated the "Realm of freedom" (*Reich der Freiheit*), in which men (mutually recognizing one another without reservation) no longer fight, and work as little as possible (Nature having been definitively mastered—that is, harmonized with Man). (159n6)

Adding a footnote in 1946, Kojève addresses the question of life at the end of history in these terms:

> What disappears is Man properly so-called—that is, Action negating the given, and Error, or in general, the Subject *opposed* to the Object. In point of fact, the end of human Time or History—that is, the definitive annihilation of Man properly so-called or of the free and historical Individual—means quite simply the cessation of Action in the full sense of the term. Practically, this means: the disappearance of wars and bloody revolutions. And also the disappearance of *Philosophy*; for since Man himself no longer changes essentially, there is no longer any reason to change the (true) principles which are at the basis of his understanding of the World and of himself. But all the rest can be preserved indefinitely; art, love, play, etc., etc.; in short, everything that makes Man *happy*. (158–159n6)

One cannot help wondering what life would be like at the end of history. Given that throughout history man has been characterized by negativity (most notably including errors, ideals, and the like), one wonders what we would become in the absence of the active negativity that grounded our freedom, individuality, and creativity. The elements of risk, of daring to confront the unknown, of innovative individuality, which seem to constitute no small part of what makes for the excitement of life and human seriousness, would no longer appear to have a place. Leo Strauss presented some reasons to Kojève in a letter of August 22, 1948, as to why he was not convinced that the Kojèvean End State either would in fact, or rationally should, satisfy human beings; as for the rest of the objections that he did not find time to develop, he evoked them by referring to the "last men" depicted by Nietzsche in *Thus Spake Zarathustra*.[4]

It is very difficult indeed to accept certain necessary concomitants of history's completion through the attainment of definitive systematic knowledge. Kojève powerfully presents this difficulty in his last lecture by giving a brief account of how hard it was for Hegel himself to come to terms with history's completion. I would like to quote from this account at length:

> The Wise Man can speak of *Science* as *his* Science only to the extent that he can speak of *death* as *his* death. For, as he proceeds to the *Logik*, the Wise Man *completely* abolishes Time—that is, History—that is, his own truly and specifically human reality, which already in the *Phenomenology* is but a *past* reality: he definitively abandons his reality as a free and historical Individual, as Subject opposed to the Object, or as Man who is essentially something other (*Anderes*) than Nature.
>
> Hegel himself knows this full well. And he knew it at least as early as 1802. For in his essay of 1802 entitled *Glauben und Wissen*, there is a passage in which he plainly says so, and which I would like to cite in ending my commentary on the *Phenomenology*. In this passage we read the following (Volume I, pages 303f.):[5]
>
> "The whole sphere of finiteness, of one's being something, of the sensual—is swallowed up in true-or-genuine Faith when confronted with the thought and intuition (*Anschauung*) of the Eternal, [thought and intuition] here becoming one and the same thing. All the gnats of Subjectivity are burned in this devouring flame, and *the very consciousness* of this giving-of-oneself (*Hingeben*) and of this annihilation (*Vernichtens*) is annihilated (*vernichtet*)."
>
> Hegel knows it and says it. But he also says, in one of his letters, that this knowledge cost him dearly. He speaks of a period of total depression that he lived through between the twenty-fifth and thirtieth years of his life: a "Hypochondria" that went "*bis zur Erlähmung aller Kräfte*," that was so severe as "to paralyze all his powers," and that came precisely from the fact that he could not accept the necessary abandonment of *Individuality*—that is, actually, of humanity—which the idea of absolute Knowledge demanded. But, finally, he surmounted this "Hypochondria." And becoming a Wise Man by that final acceptance of death, he published a few years later the First Part of the "System of Science," entitled "Science of the Phenomenology of the Spirit," in which he definitively reconciles himself with all that is and has been, by declaring that there will never more be anything new on earth. (168)

I have quoted from the end of Kojève's course at such length for two reasons. First, the subject matter: the end of history, an issue that I believe to be central for understanding Kojève's thought—and an issue on which Kojève changed his position in an important respect and which I take up again in chapter 4. Second, I should like to end my discussion of this famous seminar with some reflection on a question suggested by Raymond Aron's remarks about Kojève's seminar in the passage quoted near the beginning of this chapter. What was it about Kojève's teaching that so deeply affected and fascinated a diverse group of highly gifted intellectuals? It seems to me that this final page of Kojève's interpretation of Hegel's *Phenomenology* provides a particular text whose close interpretation enables one to gain some insight into the sources of his persuasive power.

For one thing, Kojève was immensely persuasive as an interpreter of Hegel's texts, which are remarkably difficult and dense, and filled with difficult and unfamiliar terminology. The Hegelian text of 1802 translated and interpreted toward the end of this lecture is difficult enough, but I think it fair to say that much or even most of the *Phenomenology* is more difficult. With his expansive translations (sometimes verging on paraphrases) and luminous interpretations, Kojève brought great lucidity to these puzzling Hegelian texts, and gave his listeners (and now readers) the impression of penetrating things dark and difficult so as to gain new insights of amazing power. One gets a sense of being let in to see things that are denied to most people (and to oneself before hearing Kojève).

No less important for the power of his interpretations were the profundity and importance of the themes that he treated. This concluding page, for instance, ties many of them together: the search for wisdom, human mortality, the character of historical time and action through which humanity creates itself, and the goals of human aspiration and their relation to conceptions of divinity. All are evoked in the concluding chapter of this historical phenomenological anthropology and brought into connection with the underlying metaphysical themes of history and time, nature and space, and with the ontological analysis of identity, negativity, and totality. One receives the combined impressions of depth, clarity, importance, and comprehensiveness.

Finally, Kojève manages to present the philosophic enterprise as something heroic (that is, as the highest human possibility, verging on something superhuman). On the one hand, we have seen how Kojève opens up the possibility of the philosopher's activism in moving the historical process forward. Here in contemplating the end of philosophy in its transformation into wisdom at the end of history, Kojève vividly evokes the philosopher Hegel as exemplifying a special kind of courage needed to face the profoundly difficult truth. Kojève elaborates what it means to attain wisdom. Coming to terms with the attainment of definitive knowledge involves accepting the loss of one's customary way of viewing things and experiencing life, especially in this context the attachment to freedom, the love of creativity, and the eagerness for novelty; one must even discard the sense one previously had of one's own individuality. (One might think that for Hegel, however, the consolation of being the first to cross the finish line might provide no small consolation.) Now, this theme of a kind of courage that is needed to accept the truth is, to be sure, a most time-honored theme of philosophers. It is memorably depicted in Plato's *Republic*, which develops at great length how a life fully devoted to philosophy (as philosopher-ruler) requires one to abandon all sorts of normal attachments to one's own (gold and other property, spouse, children, etc.). And even on the materialist and hedonist end of the classical spectrum of philosophy, Lucretius, while poetically emphasizing the pleasures that accompany knowing the truth (when that truth expels irrational fears and frees one from the torments of vain desires and from various other painful errors), also makes clear how wrenching and difficult it can be fully and genuinely to accept that truth, above all the fact of one's own mortality and the impermanence of all the things to which human beings can be attached and that they can love. Furthermore, the truth whose acceptance makes such demands on a person's courage or strength of soul has a powerfully paradoxical character. This is clearly the case here in Kojève's discussion of Hegel, on account of the manifestly paradoxical character of the very notion of an end of history and indeed the end of the human as we have known it. But again, the necessity of accepting upon full consideration a position that to common opinion appears paradoxical is another venerable philosophic theme. Plato here, as so often, provides a classic example: Socrates' arguments about justice in the *Gorgias* emphasize, and indeed glory in, their paradoxical character; he seems to relish announcing that virtually no one else in Athens, or elsewhere, would tend to agree with his formulations about justice and politics. The antiquity of these themes about the philosopher, however, does not, I think, diminish their power; what is noteworthy is Kojève's ability to evoke them in the altogether new context of the Hegelian argument for the full culmination of the development of philosophy into definitive wisdom.

And so Kojève's seminar ended in 1939 with his discussion of the transformation of philosophy into wisdom at the end of history. Since the attainment of wisdom is the goal at which philosophy aims, it would seem at first sight to be an unmixed blessing. In fact, the matter is somewhat more complicated, and the final lecture addresses what a human being must necessarily give up in order to accept this idea of the end of history. Despite the loss that is entailed, this acceptance is presented as fulfilling the aspiration of the philosopher as well as providing a definitive solution to the problem of recognition for all human beings. The end of history itself is not fully spelled out, but involves the definitive resolution of all conflicts, the attainment of universal satisfaction of the desire for recognition, and the promise of a continuation under a more socialized (or perhaps communist) state of all the human activities that constitute happiness into the indefinite future (no longer a historical future, dominated by negativity and change, but a postrevolutionary and posthistorical state with a full harmony of man and nature). The fullest realization of truly human life at the end of history is that of the wise man; but in a more proper sense this life should be called posthuman or divine.

The end of history as it comes to sight in *Introduction to the Reading of Hegel* presents an important ambiguity. On the one hand, Kojève states that this end has not yet been reached, that Hegel's philosophical doctrine is not yet a truth, and that the achievement of the universal and homogeneous state lies in the future as the contingent outcome of a human project. But on the other hand, in this concluding discussion, Kojève presents Hegel as actually coming to grips with the reality (not the illusion) of attaining definitive wisdom. After the war, Kojève would rethink this issue of what the end of history must be understood to mean, and I shall therefore return to the issue again in chapter 4. Meanwhile, during the war, Kojève wrote his most extensive and specific political books, which provide numerous details, especially of a political and juridical sort, that relate to this end state. It is to these writings that I shall turn in the next chapter.

NOTES

1. Judith Butler presents a thoughtful discussion of the centrality for Kojève's reading of Hegel of desire and temporality in *Subjects of Desire: Hegelian Reflections in Twentieth-Century France* (New York: Columbia University Press, 1987; paperback edition, 1999), 68–79.

2. Alternatively, one could argue that the philosopher's full articulation of the character of a fully developed historical epoch will necessarily draw people's attention to what is imperfect and unsatisfactory about that historical world, and in this way it will motivate the next wave of negating action (revolution). (To maintain this position, one would have to develop an argument about the political effectiveness of the philosopher's rhetoric.) In this interpretation, Kojève's difference from Hegel in the direction of the philosopher's activism is less than what I have stated in the text; but I prefer the view taken in the text above on account of the rather more evidently activist tone of Kojève's remarks in "Hegel, Marx, and Christianity," in his letter to Tran-Duc-Thao, and in his "Action politique des philosophes."

3. The mode of representation of reality by modern physics, however, is according to Kojève algorithmic rather than discursive.

4. This perspective on the problem of the end of history has been given its widest currency in Francis Fukuyama's *The End of History and the Last Man* (New York: Free Press, 1993).

5. Kojève refers to the Lasson-Hoffmeister edition of the complete works of Hegel (Leipzig: Felix Meiner Verlag, 1905–). Words joined together by hyphens represent translations of a single German word.

Chapter Three

Politics and Law toward the End of History

In his famous seminar on Hegel, Kojève announced the end of history, reflected on its logical necessity, and sketched with broad strokes its character as a universal and homogeneous state. During this period, Hitler's rule of Germany (and to a lesser degree Mussolini's of Italy) gave thoughtful observers grave grounds to fear that war on a massive scale lay ahead, and shortly after the end of Kojève's seminar, war did in fact break out. How did Kojève, a left-wing rationalist Hegelian committed to the end of history as the universal and homogeneous state, understand and react to the astounding political events of 1939–1945? Three writings of this period enable one to see how he came to grips with the relation of his Hegelian theory to the actual world-shattering events of that time. These writings are remarkable in two different ways: On the one hand, Kojève in no sense abandons his fundamental Hegelian position. Since, as we saw in the previous chapter, he took the position that the full working out of the end of history lay ahead in the future, still subject to contingent events, he was able to maintain his fundamental view of that end of history while trying to make sense of what was actually happening in the world. On the other hand, these writings display a remarkable flexibility in his ways of dealing with the contingencies of contemporary events. Furthermore, they show a development over time, from openness in 1942 to the notion that France under the Vichy government of Pétain might be ripe for the elaboration of some kind of revolutionary national ideal to the conviction in 1945 that the era of nations was over and that the era of empires (that is, of political entities larger than the nation-state but still short of one universal state) was now well under way.

While announcing the end of history as the universal and homogeneous state in his seminar on Hegel, Kojève had elaborated, however, precious few

47

political and legal details about this end state. As we have seen, while taking the Hegelian system as being somehow definitive knowledge in a decisive respect by completing the fundamental evolution of philosophy, Kojève nonetheless held that in the real world, the perfected State, the universal and homogeneous state, had not yet arrived, so that Hegel's teaching remained in some sense an ideal rather than the truth, that is, the discursive revelation of reality. Given this important qualification on his endorsement of Hegelianism as completed wisdom, it is no surprise that Kojève did not take Hegelian teachings on the state, on right, on authority, as the final word; nor, therefore, did he limit himself to the enterprise of interpreting the Hegelian texts. Instead, he continued to develop his own thinking by writing, during the war, his own analyses of political, moral, and juridical phenomena.

From this wartime period three interesting writings, all published posthumously, merit discussion. The first to be written is the last to have been published: a manuscript dated May 16, 1942, and entitled *La Notion de l'Autorité* (*The Notion of Authority*, hereafter referred to as *Authority*).[1] Published in the year 2004 in Gallimard's Bibliothèque des Idées series, edited and presented by François Terré, it contains about 150 pages of Kojève (along with a forty-five-page presentation by Terré). The second, and by far the longest writing at nearly six hundred pages, is *Esquisse d'une Phénoménologie du Droit: Exposé Provisoire* (*Outline of a Phenomenology of Right: Provisional Exposition*, hereafter referred to as *Right*), written during the summer of 1943.[2] Third, a brief writing dated August 27, 1945, is entitled "L'Empire Latin: Esquisse d'une doctrine de la politique française" ("Latin Empire: Outline of a Doctrine of French Policy," hereafter referred to as "Empire"); it first appeared in somewhat abridged form in the first, May 1990, issue of the thrice-yearly periodical edited by Bernard-Henri Lévy, *La Règle du Jeu* (*The Rule of the Game*), and is thirty-five pages long.[3]

These three writings are very different indeed from Kojève's commentary on Hegel's *Phenomenology of Spirit*. In fact, they are not at all commentaries on or interpretation of Hegel. Kojève pursues his own line of thought with great flexibility in relation to the Hegelian system. He works within a basically Hegelian framework, to be sure, in terms of the fundamental importance of history; human freedom in the strong sense of creativity, including self-creativity; the crucial importance of the master-slave dialectic, fighting, and work; and the universal and homogeneous state as the goal of history. But within this framework, Kojève displays a remarkable kind and degree of openness regarding certain details of the end state and especially regarding what the specific path of history might be on the way toward that ultimate Kojèvean-Hegelian goal.

The *Outline of a Phenomenology of Right*, as one expects from the title, proceeds on the level of phenomenology, with the same understanding of phenomenology and using the same phenomenological method of rationally ordered description that Kojève had set forth as Hegel's in *Introduction*. The other two writings are also phenomenological, although in *Authority* he develops his argument, albeit quite briefly, on the metaphysical level as well and also gives an extremely brief reference to the need, for completeness, to add an ontological analysis. "Empire" most fully merits the term "outline" or "sketch." In sketching an overall policy or a grand strategy for France, Kojève here argues on the level of the historical phenomena, but with less of an effort to be comprehensive or to show a rationally necessary ordering of the phenomena. From this overall characterization of the approach taken in these three works, it is clear that Kojève maintained the most basic element of Hegelian thought as he understood it: the conception of philosophical discourse as necessarily developing itself on the three levels of phenomenology, metaphysics, and ontology. Indeed, in *Authority*, he makes an interesting suggestion of philosophical method: that the way to develop the correctness of one's philosophical discourse, and so to advance toward completeness on all three levels, is to move back and forth between these levels: to descend from an ontology (taken as definitive) toward the phenomenon; to ascend from a phenomenology (taken as definitive) toward Being as Being (*Authority*, 134).

Early in *Right*, Kojève sets forth some details of his phenomenological approach. He likens it to Socratic-Platonic conversational inquiry into what something is, to Aristotle's way of formulating definitions, or to Max Weber's notion of the elaboration of "ideal types." In seeking to define a basic phenomenon of human life, such as the juridical, the political, the religious, or the moral, one typically observes that a clear definition is not available, in the sense of being widely known and generally accepted; one finds instead a variety of competing definitions. To arrive at a correct definition of the phenomenon, one needs to survey all the ways in which the term in question is used. All of these uses can most likely not be brought under one definition. One must then begin by examining an especially clear, evident, characteristic example of the phenomenon and on that basis formulate a definition. One then proceeds to compare that definition with other clear and characteristic examples; this process will probably lead to clarifications and corrections of the definition. Eventually one may come to what seems an adequate definition. Then one must test this definition against, in principle, all examples of the use of the term (and of synonymous and related terms). To take the example of juridical phenomena, one will in some cases find a phenomenon often called "juridical" that is not covered by one's definition; if one's definition is correct, one must be able to explain why the phenomenon in question is often mistaken for a juridical one. Conversely, one may come upon a phenomenon that is often not called juridical but that should be so called according to one's definition; in that case one must be able to explain what about that phenomenon causes its juridical character often to be overlooked. When one cannot do this, one must continue the process of refining one's definition.

One may well at first blush feel surprise that a modern left Hegelian should characterize phenomenological inquiry in this Socratic-sounding manner, and one may wonder whether Kojève is falling back toward ancient philosophy. In fact, he is not. Ancient philosophy seeks insight into eternal, unchanging essences in nature, so as to articulate, for instance, what the eternally grounded character of right or justice is; for a Platonist, therefore, the truth of what something is must inhere in its relation to some eternal being. Kojève as Hegelian seeks to articulate a definition of something, for instance right, that is temporally changing, that has a history of change. A definition may succeed in designating a whole class of phenomena, for example the juridical, in an abstract or formal way; but the substantive content and the details of that phenomenon change over time. Genuine knowledge is not limited to the definition, but must proceed to give a full account of all the realizations in the world of that definition over time; genuine knowledge is possible if and only if the totality of temporal changes can be grasped as constituting an intelligible whole.

AUTHORITY

Kojève introduces his inquiry into authority with the observation that this phenomenon has been little studied, even though it is manifestly crucial for understanding political life or the State. In fact, Kojève suggests that admitting that every State presupposes and rests on authority, one could deduce the theory of the State from the theory of authority. Authority has, to be sure, been discussed by most political thinkers, but no one has produced a thorough, comprehensive account of the essence of the phenomenon. Kojève identifies four types of theories of authority: the theological or theocratic account of authority; Plato's theory that authority rests on the eternal idea of justice; Aristotle's theory of authority based on wisdom, prudence, or forethought; and Hegel's theory of the Master and Slave. Only this last theory, according to Kojève, has been adequately developed on the phenomenological, metaphysical, and ontological levels. But all four theories, including Hegel's, suffer the defect of being exclusive: they develop a theory of one type of authority and wrongly take it for the whole of authority. Kojève's identification of Hegel's incompleteness on this matter of authority is, in my judgment, his most serious critique of Hegel's system within the political/moral realm of human history. Kojève, of course, proposes to remedy this defect through his own comprehensive analysis.

Authority is manifestly a social phenomenon involving interaction, and authority belongs to an active person or an agent in the proper sense of the term (who as such must be free and conscious). Kojève's most basic definition of authority seeks to define it from the outside, externally, as something revealed by the observable behavior of two human actors. The authoritative act is characterized by its not being opposed by the person or persons toward whom it is directed, who could oppose it but consciously and voluntarily refrain from opposition. When one person, who has the possibility of acting otherwise, acts in accordance with the direction of another, the latter is shown to have authority over the former. Kojève sums up his definition of authority with three equivalent formulations: Authority is an agent's possibility of acting on others (or another) without the others' reacting on him, even though they are capable of doing so. Alternatively, in acting with authority, the agent can change the external human given without suffering anything in response, that is, without himself changing as a function of his action. Or finally, authority is the possibility of acting without making any compromise (in the broad sense of the term). Authority differs fundamentally from force: if one has authority, the mere expression of one's will suffices to cause the other to act; one precisely does not need to use force to compel the other to do one's will. The use of force or compulsion displays the absence of authority. Likewise, if one must persuade, or in some way come to a compromise, to bring about the action one wills, one's authority is absent or at least imperfect.

Kojève further clarifies the notion of authority by exploring its relationship to *Droit* (right, legality, legitimacy, justice), love, and the Divine. Authority and Right are affiliated phenomena, which differ in their differing relationships to the use of force. The affiliation is clear from Kojève's defining assertion that I have the right to something when I can do it without encountering opposition (or reaction), such opposition being in principle possible. The difference is that, as regards authority, the possible reaction remains in the realm of mere possibility; if it becomes actual, the authority is not really there. In the case of Right, however, the reaction against it may become actual, but Right prevails if the reaction that would negate Right is prevented through the action of enforcers of Right (judge, police, etc.). In fact, the real existence of Right requires such enforcement as is needed. Right may have authority; when Right is authoritative, it holds sway without counteraction. But if Right is opposed, it can be, and needs to be, upheld by force (whereas the need for force displays the absence or defect of authority).

As regards love, the lover freely acts to do what the beloved wishes, what will please the beloved, and so one speaks, loosely, of the beloved's authority over the lover. But in fact, the lover acts spontaneously, without the beloved's actually needing to intervene or act (e.g., to command), and so the phenomena of authority and love are distinct. Their similarity, however, finds expression in some tendency to love those whose authority one recognizes and to think of something like authority as belonging to the object of love.

We would all naturally tend to recognize the authority of the Divine and even to take the Divine as the highest authority. It is possible, to be sure, to preserve that usage of the term. Kojève, however, finds that the only truly satisfactory definition of the Divine is that which can act on me but on which I cannot react. He gives the nice illustration that, when people thought that stars influenced our lives and that we could in no way act on them, they held stars to be divine; but when modern physics taught that the stars are part of a universal system of acting and reacting matter, they—and indeed the natural world as a whole—came no longer to be considered divine. If one cannot in principle react against the Divine, then divine "authority" exceeds the definition of human authority; in Kojève's definition, (human) authority *could* always be opposed, but those recognizing it *choose* not to do so. Divine "authority" is authority *minus* the possibility of reacting against it, or better, *plus* the irresistible power of the holder of authority. Needless to say, people have often held a view of gods that does not measure up to Kojève's definition or ideal type of the Divine—one need only think of Achilles' attempt to fight Apollo or the river god. In any case, men have generally attributed the maximum of authority to the Divine and sought to clothe human authority with attributes of divinity.

But whereas divine "authority" is irresistible, eternal, and hence free of all risk, human authority can be resisted and therefore always involves risk—at the very least the risk that authority itself might be lost and sometimes (especially when change of political regime or the holding of supreme power is at stake) even the risk that the former holder of authority might lose his life. One *could* react against the action of any human authority, but in recognizing that authority one consciously and voluntarily renounces the possible reaction against it. Why does one renounce opposition? One must have some reason for it. Human authority therefore presents causes, reasons, justifications for itself as authority, and the exploration of these leads to the analysis of the pure types of authority, filling in the formal abstract definition with substantive content.

Kojève argues that there are in fact four basic pure types of authority: the authority of the Father, of the Leader (*le Chef*), of the Master, and of the Judge. Each of these has been especially well analyzed by one of the four theories present in the philosophic tradition already mentioned, but each type of authority was mistakenly presented as the only one or the decisive one. When one reflects on these four types, one might well ask how one could know that typology to be complete and adequate. Kojève seeks to provide assurance on this point through presenting a much briefer metaphysical analysis, which relates each pure type of authority to one of the three modes of time or to Eternity taken as opposed to time as such.

One type of authority is that of the master over the slave; variants of this are the authority of noble over commoner, military over civilian, man over woman, and victor over vanquished. Kojève holds that Hegel developed this theory of authority thoroughly, referring the reader for more details to his own article "Autonomy and Dependence of Self-Consciousness."[4] In a fight between equals purely for the sake of recognition, in which life is put at risk for a nonbiological end, the future master displays willingness to fight to the death; the future slave, overcome by fear of death, recognizes the superiority of the master and submits to his authority. Choosing not to endure the risk of his life, the slave thus consciously and voluntarily renounces his possibility of reacting against the master's action, and this is to recognize the master's authority. It is worth emphasizing that this authority arises from risk: from the differential willingness to endure the risk of death. It does not and cannot arise simply from great power or force, because as Kojève has emphasized, the use of force manifests the absence of authority (the point here is analogous to Rousseau's argument that strength or force cannot create right, that there is no "right of the stronger").

Since Hegel in Kojève's judgment did not elaborate any other theory of authority, he appears to have thought that this one kind was at the root of all. Kojève strongly disagrees, turning next to the authority of the leader of a band or group. A master, while holding authority as master over his slaves, may hold authority as leader in relationship to many masters in a political community. Some of the variants of this authority of the leader of a group include the authority of the superior over the inferior (of director over employee, of the officer over the enlisted man), the teacher's authority over the student, and the authority of knowledgeable experts, technicians, soothsayers, prophets, and so forth. This authority of leader is of a basically different character from that of a master, and it was correctly described by Aristotle. Aristotle (wrongly) presented his theory as though it were one of natural mastery over natural slaves and hence as a theory of mastery; it is in fact the theory of leadership. According to Aristotle, the master's right to exercise authority over the slave comes from his foresight and prudence. Under the master's authority the slave will live better and more reasonably than he could do on his own, because of his defective intelligence and prudence. This theory of the master's authority in fact analyzes the authority of the leader whose plans, projects, intelligence, and foresight are accepted as authoritative by his fellows. And Aristotle does say explicitly, in conformity with this theory of authoritative leadership, that *phronēsis* (prudence or good sense and forethought) is the distinctive virtue of the ruler, in which the ruled as such need not have a share.

Since both Aristotle and Hegel, each in his own way, appear, in Kojève's account, to have extended one theory to the two differing types of authority of master and leader, one suspects that these two types may stand close to each other or that the distinction between them may be in some respects subtle or difficult to sustain. That this is the case as a practical matter appears when Kojève later turns to political applications of his theory, for in his view it turns out that governmental authority tends necessarily to unite the authority of master and that of leader.

A third pure type of authority is that of the judge, the variants of which include the authority of the just or honest man, of the arbiter or arbitrator, of the controller or auditor or censor, and of the confessor. This authority comes neither from risk and conquest nor from foresight and projects but from justice and equity. The judge does not propose a project or display special forethought; it is not his vaster knowledge of the laws but his justice that founds his authority as judge. This theory was fully elaborated by Plato as the theory of all authority: genuine authority comes from justice or equity; any other source of so-called authority is illegitimate and therefore unstable and not altogether real as authority. For Kojève this claim is clearly false in its exclusivity; the leader's authority is not simply founded in justice, and indeed the authority of justice can conflict with the authority of the master, the leader, or the father; but the existence of such conflicts does indeed provide support to the claim that the authority of justice is *sui generis* and independent of those others.

Kojève finds a story of Herodotus (Book I, chapter 96–100) especially revealing of the character of the authority of justice. When the Medes were living in a state of great disorder and injustice (a kind of Hobbesean war of all against all), Deioces decided to practice justice. People began to come to him to have their differences settled, and his authority as judge grew. Eventually he was so busy with judging that he refused to take on the settlement of any additional cases, saying that he needed to attend to his own affairs; the Medes prevailed on him to continue as judge by conferring on him in addition the power of king. From this story one sees a twofold truth: that justice to prevail reliably and durably in the affairs of men does normally require the assistance of political power; but also that justice does have its own authority, proven by its possibility of generating itself spontaneously. A person's justice, equity, fairness, and impartiality tend of themselves to generate authority.

The fourth authority is that of the Father; its variants are the authority of the older over the younger, the authority of tradition, the authority of someone dead (through his testament), and the authority of an author over his work. Kojève notes that one naturally expects that the fourth theory, the scholastic theory of theological or theocratic authority, will correspond to this authority of the Father, but he concedes that the correspondence is not immediately or simply apparent. A complication arises from the fact that the scholastic elaboration of divine authority attributes, not surprisingly, all kinds of authority to God: God is master of us all; surely he is leader, of his chosen people if not of all, toward a better future; and divine justice and judgment is a fundamentally important aspect and power of divinity. But, according to Kojève's analysis, these pure types of authority of the master, the leader, and the judge are adequately accounted for by the other theories, of Hegel, Aristotle, and Plato. If the scholastic, theological tradition is of interest to us in its discussions of divine authority, it would be for its account of the authority of the Father, and of course God's authority is also that of the Father of us all, our heavenly Father. While divine authority includes all four types, it is God as Father, God as Creator, as source or cause of our being, that seems to be fundamental and distinctive. The basic source of the Father's authority is the authority of cause over effect. The cause holds authority over the effect because not to recognize such authority is in a sense to deny oneself. The Father's authority, as explicated theologically, emerges most powerfully in the conception of God as Creator, which comes fully into its own in the Judeo-Christian and Islamic theologies; partial aspects of it, however, are to be found to some degree in any theology. The cause transmits something of itself, perhaps even its essence, to the effect; it is natural thus to think of such authority as transmitted by heredity. Indeed hereditary transmission characterizes both the authority of the human father and divine authority (most fully developed in the doctrine of divine right of kings). As for the variants, Kojève comments that the authority of the old over the young rests on the view that the previous generation is responsible for the next; similarly tradition is understood as causing us to be what we are and so to have authority for us. Perhaps the most complete example of authority is that of the author over his work, and Kojève's examples show that he takes *author* in a broad sense, to include the authority of the founder of a philosophical, artistic, or literary school; the authority of the founder of a colony; and the authority of Baden-Powell over the Boy Scouts.

These four pure types of authority rarely exist in their full purity. As we saw regarding the authority of the judge in the story from Herodotus, the purest actualization of the type is the arbiter whose authority depends solely on his reputation for justice. But such authority is rather limited in scope and in duration; the more stable and enduring authority of the judge requires the added support of laws and state institutions. Most real examples of authority tend to combine two, three, or all four pure types. Permutations within each combination are also relevant (for instance, the combination of judge and leader would have two variants, depending on which pure type predominated in the combination). Accordingly, there would be four pure types; six combinations of two types, with two permutations of each combination, for a total of twelve; four combinations of three types, with six permutations of each combination for a total of twenty-four; and twenty-four permutations of the one combination of all four pure types; for a grand total of sixty-four possibilities, in principle. Doubtless some of these do not exist in reality, and doubtless too the distinctions between some of them are too subtle to be useful. In any case, Kojève makes no attempt to deal with them exhaustively, but gives just a few examples, most interestingly in his discussion of the political applications of his theory of authority.

He speaks also of the genesis and transmission of the various types of authority. Each pure type of authority can be generated spontaneously. The master generates his authority over the slave through putting his life at risk; the leader convinces people of his foresight or persuades them to pursue his project; the judge, as we have seen, acquires authority through his reputation for impartiality and fairness. Each of these three types generates authority through some distinctive excellence. In contrast, the father's authority is of a sort that every man may possess. Kojève argues that certain events that might easily be taken to be the creation of authority are in fact better understood as cases of its transmission. When people elect a leader, are they creating authority? Kojève argues otherwise: the (future) leader, through his proposals and projects (normally supported by his past accomplishments), has spontaneously won authority for himself; the people's election is better understood as a manifestation of this authority.

If Kojève's account of authority is adequate, it must be able to account for all commonly recognized types by showing how they are one combination or another of his four pure types. Of particular interest is his discussion, in which he explicitly refers several times to Rousseau's analysis in *On the Social Contract*, of some obviously politically relevant types of authority: that of the majority, of the minority, and of the general will. Something like an authority of the majority exists, and finds expression in appeals, for instance, to public opinion, to "What would people say?" and the like. But the minority also appeals to something like an opposite kind of authority, manifested in snobbism, the superiority of the original over the banal, and other displays of deference toward the opinion of some allegedly elite minority. These two "authorities" are not real authority: they stand at opposition to each other and neither has real (i.e., recognized and effective) authority over the other. Now in fact, for Kojève, the majority simply as majority does not have authority; it has superior force (as John Locke explicitly notes in his *Civil Government*), but force (or the believable threat of such force) is as we have seen something different from authority. Nor does the minority have any authority simply as minority; if the minority claims authority in some way, it is through appealing to some qualitative superiority that generates authority of one of the four types already analyzed (for instance, the claim to superior judgment that the few may allege as grounds for their claim to rule, as in Aristotle's analysis).

A genuine authority is that of the general will, clearly analyzed and labeled by Rousseau, but in fact recognized in various ways wherever and whenever "raison d'état" is appealed to or the State's authority is viewed as somehow sacred. Kojève agrees with Rousseau's clear distinction between the general will and the will of the majority; he elaborates, with Rousseau, that the authority of the general will is the authority not of one part over another but of the whole over the parts. When the general will lost its divine attributes, the authority of the majority was erroneously appealed to (and replaced later, Kojève notes, by other "supports" for the general will: Lenin-Stalin's "Proletariat," Mussolini's "Impero," and Hitler's "Volk") (*Authority*, 105). Kojève proceeds to examine what kind of authority this authority of the general will as that of whole over parts really is. From the consideration that the authority of whole over parts makes sense only within the context of a whole that is a living organism, he concludes that the most fundamental level of such authority is a variant of the Father's authority, the authority of the guarantor of identity and continuity with the past. Combined with this is the whole's authority to provide for the harmonious relationship among the parts, which — as in Plato's famous formulation in the *Republic*—is the authority of justice. The general will thus provides an authority of the F/J (father/judge) type. The authority of leader is missing from this authority of whole over parts; its absence is reflected in the fact that innovation, projects for the future, leadership, come not from the whole as such but are proposed by individuals or parts. Accordingly, in Rousseau's account, the legislator who proposes a new code of legislation for the whole society is an individual who must generate his own authority as leader, while he as such cannot represent the general will and has no share of the authority of the whole. I imagine that in this context Kojève thought also of the authority acquired by the vanguard of the proletariat.

Regarding the transmission of authority, the three modes are heredity, nomination, and election. Heredity, of course, seems natural enough in the case of the father; in most applications, however, hereditary transmission rests on a kind of primitive or magical view of certain virtues being thus transmitted. Any authority could be transmitted hereditarily (as it was with divine right monarchy), but it seems for the most part irrational and especially inappropriate as regards the authority of the judge (where impartiality is crucial). Accordingly, one frequently sees examples of judicial authority coming to be ad hoc by the lot (as in jury selection). Regarding nomination and election, which are often confused in ordinary usage, Kojève finds it useful to make a distinction. Nomination is the transmission of authority by one who has an authority of the same type to another who is to receive that same kind of authority. Election is transmission or bestowal of an authority that those making the election do not themselves have, for instance when the popular assembly elects a leader. In this respect, choice by lot and choice by voting are both modes of election.

Arguing on the metaphysical level, Kojève affirms that authority is a distinctively human, social, historical phenomenon. In accordance with his Hegelian standpoint, then, authority can manifest itself only in a world that has a temporal structure (and Kojève evokes distinctively human time as having the rhythm future → past → present; as opposed to the "natural" times in which the present takes primacy in the domain of physics and in which the past takes primacy in the domain of biology).[5] Since human time is characterized by primacy of the future, the authority of the leader holds primacy: "The authority par excellence is that of the 'revolutionary' (political, religious, etc.) Leader who has a *universal* 'project' (Stalin)" (*Authority*, 118–119). (The reader of *Introduction* is not surprised to see Kojève give Stalin as *the* example of the leader.)

On the metaphysical level, Kojève asserts that each mode of time holds some sort of authority. Kojève relates each pure type of authority to one of the three modes of time or to Eternity taken as opposed to time as such. The authority of the judge stands apart from that of father, master, and leader: the judge does not act, but from a contemplative standpoint passes judgment on the actions of all others. He appeals to nothing temporal: his just judgment does not appeal to present interests or fixed positions based on the past or desires for the future, but rather to eternal principles or standards of justice applicable to past, present, and future. Kojève's argument for basing the judge's authority on a relation to Eternity, to eternal principles of justice, seems puzzling at first, given his critique of Platonism as unable to give an adequate account of how eternal being is accessible to our thinking (which necessarily takes place in time). The puzzle is cleared up by noting that Kojève does not take Eternity as something that really exists outside of time to which the judge has access or which somehow can intervene in time. Rather he suggests that the eternal (in relation to the human world) is to be understood as defining itself as the negation of temporality as such, as opposition to all three modes of time, as judging unjust actions of any type on the basis of their deviation from unchanging principles of justice and right. Now, of course the content of the principles of justice develops over history, as Kojève was to elaborate in detail in his next writing, *Phenomenology of Right*. But eternal justice, in the sense of just principles standing against the fluctuating motives of temporal actions, is what underlies the judge's authority, which can thus be said to manifest a metaphysical basis of Eternity.

The other types of authority rest on the three modes of time. The past has a certain authority: the past tends to be venerable; a kind of sanctity belongs to the traditional and to the old. The authority of the past is not of mere past as such—as Kojève notes, a rock may be very ancient yet has no authority—but comes from the human past that is relevant to the human reality, that is, the past as cause of the present, the past as tradition that shapes our reality. The authority of the father, of tradition, of the cause over the effect, is the type of authority that rests metaphysically on the past. The future has an authority as well: just as in some ways the old hold authority, in others the young, the rising generation, the hope of the future, partake of authority. It is the leader who represents the claim and authority of the Future, in his appeal to the project, the creation of a new order, the attainment of hitherto unattained goals. Finally, the present too has a kind of authority: everyone wishes to be "up to date" (as Kojève puts it, in English) and not to lag behind the times. Again, the present as authoritative is not just the present as such. After all, every reality is by definition present, including realities that have authority, realities that have none, and realities that submit to the authority of another. The present as authoritative is not the $t = 0$ of physics but the human, historical present, linked to the past, acting toward the future. Now, action opposes given, present being; it asserts something and negates something else in the present. Action in the strong sense puts the present reality at risk; therefore the archetype of such authoritative being in the present is the master, whose authority is founded in risk. The master's authority is of one who acts masterfully in the present, who masters the present danger or necessity. "The authority of the 'present need' opposed to that of the 'dream of the future' and of the 'preservation of the past' is, in the final analysis, the Authority of the necessities of *war* or, generally speaking, of the *vital risks* that accompany the penetration of a Nation's Past into its Future *through* its Present" (*Authority*, 128).

Through this brief metaphysical analysis, Kojève seeks confirmation that the fourfold phenomenological analysis of authority is adequate and complete. He completes this metaphysical sketch by suggesting that Eternity realizes itself as formal cause (which manifests itself in the human world as the disinterested, contemplative standpoint of the judge). The present manifests itself as efficient cause (the present action in the proper sense of the term, the master); the future manifests itself as final cause (action projected into the future, the leader); and the past manifests itself as material cause (tradition, existential memory, traditional action that is effectuated by a kind of inertia, the father).

Admitting that his metaphysical discussion is but a sketch and the ontological completion of the argument is lacking, Kojève turns to some political
applications of his analysis of authority. His relatively long and complex discussion is most interesting, in my judgment, in its treatment of the division of
powers taught by the social contract and constitutional traditions and in its inquiry into the political problem of the authority of the father, of the past, and
of tradition.

Political authority, the authority of the State, may arise in a number of possible ways: in Locke's phrase, for instance, a father may become the "politic
monarch" of an extended family; or a judge may acquire kingly authority in addition, as in Herodotus' tale. Whatever its first origin, political authority tends
to include all four pure types of authority. Medieval scholastic teachings of the
divine right of kings display this full extent of political authority. Even in this
context, however, calls for independence of the judicial power arose, as exemplified by the Magna Carta; in this way the fact was manifested that the judge's
authority, rooted in Eternity, stands apart from the three temporal authorities,
which more easily go together, of father, master, and leader. The medieval
teaching of the full extent of political authority is complicated and undermined
by the existence of an unresolved conflict, namely that arising between ecclesiastical and state power, between Pope and Emperor, on account of the failure
to work out an adequate distinction between the political and the ecclesiastical
realms. The teaching of absolutism by thinkers such as Bodin and Hobbes resolved this conflict through a unified teaching of sovereignty that removed independent theological authority from the political realm. In reaction to actual
and potential abuses of absolutism, constitutional teachings arose (often resting on the working hypothesis of a "social contract") and developed—most famously in Montesquieu—a doctrine of "separation of powers." This new tradition focused its attention on dividing and balancing political power, with a
view to restricting it from despotic or tyrannical excess.

Kojève makes the astute and fascinating observation that in this development from absolutism to constitutionalism, the authority of the father silently
drops out of the picture, without any detailed analysis or discussion; political
authority comes to be discussed as a combination of the authorities of judge,
leader, and master, viewed as judicial power, legislative power, and executive
power. In this connection, Kojève makes the conservative or traditionalist
Hegelian suggestion that, with the authority of the father dropped from the
political realm, the political authority, disconnected from its past, will have a
tendency toward constant change. His formulation is striking:

Political authority from which the member "Father" has been amputated necessarily becomes, to the extent that it remains *political*, above all an authority of

Leader (of the type L→(M,J) or L→(J,M)). It is thus that "constitutional" theory, in and by its "bourgeois" revolutionary *realization*, necessarily ends in the "Dictatorship" of a Napoleon or of a Hitler. But since the Present, deprived of the past, must necessarily imply the Future in order to be human, or rather political, the Leader-Dictator must always represent a *"revolutionary* project" in course of execution. Thus, the logical ending of a Montesquieu's "constitutional" theory is a Trotsky's theory of "permanent revolution." (*Authority*, 144)

The authority of the judge (related to Eternity taken as opposed to time in its three modes) can have a certain harmonious stability in balanced opposition with the three types of authority corresponding to the three modes of time; but when the authority of the past (the father) is removed, Kojève argues, the relation of judge to leader and master is unbalanced. The authority of the judge, standing against the governmental authority of leader and master, is no longer representative of a balanced whole and tends therefore (as Marx correctly argued) to become a justice based not on the whole but on one class. For Kojève, one cannot in the long term successfully separate the political authority of leader and master. A pure leader's authority, in its separation from past and present, would be utopian, unable to realize its plans in action; a master's authority isolated in the present and looking to no future would degenerate into pure administration and technique, ultimately based on force and thus no longer a genuine authority. Governmental authority, to endure with stability, should consist of the compound of leader and master (L/M or M/L). A theoretically defensible separation of power, then, would not be legislative, executive, judicial, but the pure authority of fathers (F), the compound governmental authority of leader and master (L/M or M/L), and the pure authority of the judge (J).

Kojève does not elaborate much on this remarkable, conservative proposition that sound political theory calls for an element of the fathers' authority. He makes clear, of course, that he has in mind such paternal authority as political, as existing within a whole political authority; he does not refer to an authority of the father that would stand in opposition to political authority, as happened in the past, memorably depicted in Greek tragedies such as Sophocles' *Antigone*. He suggests that one way to achieve that goal might be to associate an element of that paternal authority with, for example, the authority of the leader (for instance, by having fathers of families constitute the legislative). But if, as modern circumstances give every indication of requiring, that possibility is obsolete (given the need to include women, single persons, and others on equal terms), he suggests a separate institution as the basis or "support" of this "paternal" authority—something like the Roman Senate, performing the function of censor. (A Senate, of course, like a *Gerousia* in Greek, derives etymologically from old age and was originally composed of old fathers.) What would such an institution do in a modern state? Kojève's tantalizing suggestion elaborates no details, but in the spirit of his remarks about France in the appendices of this book on authority (and in his discussion three years later of a possible Latin Empire), I would suggest that a Senate/censor might act to preserve and propagate traditional elements of the spirit of the nation (or Empire) and its way of life, cultural traditions, perhaps even traditional public religious observances insofar as they can be preserved without overturning the state's modern secularist basis.

It is remarkable to find this insistence on linkage with the past at the same time that Kojève maintains his leftist Hegelian interpretation of history, for here in a fascinating "Note on the events of 1848 (France)" (*Authority*, 144–145), he restates an unmistakably Marxist view (updated, to be sure): 1789–1848 was the period of bourgeois *revolution*; 1848–1940 was the period of bourgeois *domination*. During the earlier period, the bourgeoisie turned against the past and toward the future. But in 1848 the future was claimed by another class, or more precisely, "the Future intervenes into the Present in the form of a different 'revolutionary project' from that of '89." Rejecting this new revolutionary project, the bourgeoisie after 1848 turned against the future as well as the past. Shut up in the present, the bourgeoisie sustained a relation to past and future that no longer had active value, but only a virtual, ideal, that is to say purely "aesthetic" or "artistic" presence, which Kojève characterizes as "tradition vegetating in the form of 'Romanticism,' and the Revolution of 'futurism.'" Thus on the one hand Kojève clearly still looks in a Marxist manner to a future postbourgeois revolutionary project, and indeed, it seems, looks for it to take a decisive step forward in 1940; but on the other hand, he argues (as against the constitutional tradition and, even more so, against typical Marxists) for the fundamental necessity that political authority should continue or rather reconstitute an element of the authority of the father, of the past, of tradition.

Instead of continuing to extend the political applications of his analysis of authority at length in a systematic manner, Kojève concludes *Authority* with two noteworthy appendices that apply his theory to the contemporary case of Vichy France: one an "Analysis of the Authority of the *Maréchale* [Pétain]"; the other "Remarks on National Revolution." Kojève presents considerable details on the actual emergence of Pétain's authority; he discusses how in its spontaneous generation after the French defeat, it drew on all four pure types, and he reflects on what is growing and what is diminishing in the authority of the *Maréchale* and his government at the moment of his writing (May 1942). The other appendix argues that France is ready for national revolution in a general situational way but has not yet been presented with the necessary revolutionary idea. Kojève makes some rather sketchy proposals concerning the possibilities of an idea of national revolution, or at least the simulation of such an idea, for France in the present (1942) context, chiefly suggestions for political institutions embodying the various dimensions of political authority. Given his continuing Marxism, including his earlier reference to Stalin as the leader par excellence, all this concern with French national possibilities is rather surprising. Without claiming to understand it fully, I would suggest that it shows that Kojève takes the element of contingency in history very seriously indeed; he is altogether open to whatever political situation might come along and prepared to make amazingly flexible suggestions to deal with present realities, in the effort eventually to shape them toward the Hegelian or Marxist future to the realization of which he is still committed. In particular, here he seems to be sketching how France under Pétain might reorder itself in the face of continued German successes, how one could articulate a "revolutionary national idea" for France and develop new political institutions to realize it. In the circumstances of 1942, he remains open to the possibility that, for the time, a national political project may yet be what is required. But by 1945, Germany having been defeated, he would take the position, as we shall see, that the era of political action on the national scale, on the basis of the nation-state, was over.

RIGHT

Kojève's *Outline of a Phenomenology of Right* is developed in much fuller detail and at greater length than *Authority*, although even in this heavy tome Kojève explicitly underlines the partial and provisional character of his analysis; in particular here he remains almost entirely on the phenomenological level, as the title suggests. The overall Hegelian framework and the end goal of a universal and homogeneous state (which he sometimes here calls Empire) loom larger than in the *Authority*. Kojève states with complete clarity and explicitness here that the universal and homogeneous state does not exist, that it is a matter of contingency whether humanity will attain it or not, and that the details of what the ultimate *droit* will be in it can therefore not be fully given. Nonetheless, he provides an overall account of the matter. The book consists of three parts: the first deals with *droit* as such, the second with its origin and development in history, and the third with the systematic ordering of *droit* in all its parts and fields of application.

Before proceeding further, I must briefly discuss the French term *droit*, which one can best, but imperfectly, translate *right*. The full title of the book, of course, is *Esquisse d'une phénoménologie du droit: Exposé provisoire*, that is, *Outline [or Sketch] of a Phenomenology of Right: Provisional Exposition*.

Elsewhere than in the title of the book, the English translators have kept the French word *droit*, because of the difficulty of translating it. The difficulty reminds one of the problem Hobbes found in the use of the words *law* and *right* (in Latin *lex* and *jus*); Hobbes thought these two words should be clearly defined and distinguished from each other, but found that in fact they often overlapped in ways that caused difficulty for clear understanding. In French, the words *droit* and *loi* correspond to *jus* and *lex*, and English does not have one word that is commonly used in as broad a way as *droit* or *jus*; I can most easily exemplify the difficulty by pointing out that a French law school is called *école de droit*. *Droit*, in short, can mean right, law, legal system, the just or juridical, and so forth. I shall use the term "right" for *droit* wherever possible in my discussion, but where that does not work, I shall have recourse to the French term.

Kojève's phenomenological analysis begins with the articulation of a universally valid behavioral definition of right. Since this approach seems at first cumbersome and lengthy, it is worth reflecting on why he does so. We all have a sense of what right is, but it is one of those difficult concepts, like many fundamental concepts about human life, that are hard to pin down, because of how important it is, how much is at stake, how deeply we feel about it, and also (from the Hegelian standpoint) because of fundamental changes in specific content over time. In consequence, our most frequently used ways of elaborating right are likely to lead to divergence of opinion. Kojève starts from the behavioral or external approach in order to try to have a sound beginning in identifying the phenomenon to be analyzed further; accordingly he tries to find a formalistic criterion, an externally observable behavior in an objectively determinable situation, which can capture all cases of right or of the existence of a "juridical situation." The ordinary way of talking about right, which relies heavily on introspective language for its content (most fundamentally by referring juridical action to a conception of justice), will be filled in later.

His search for this universal abstract external definition produces this preliminary finding or "first behavioral definition of *droit*": "The phenomenon of '*Droit*' (in its 'behaviorist' aspect) is the intervention of an impartial and disinterested human being [C], which is necessarily carried out at the time of an interaction between two human beings, A and B, and which annuls B's reaction to A's action" (*Right*, 40). In such a situation A has the right to act as he does (subjective right), and the grounds for C's intervention can be formulated in a proposition that is a rule of right or a legal rule (objective right or law). Several logically connected legal rules may constitute a juridical doctrine that applies to a set of correlative social actions that may be called a juridical institution (for instance, marriage or insurance). The totality of such

legal rules or juridical institutions valid in a given society is called the national *droit* (system of right and legal institutions) of this society. Finally, "the
totality of all the 'legal rules' (or 'juridical institutions') which have been
valid . . . in different societies in the course of universal history constitutes the
phenomenon of '*Droit*' as such" (*Right*, 41).

After this first definition, Kojève analyzes and discusses each of its parts
in considerable detail, expanding or refining it so as ultimately to come up
with a "Second 'Behaviorist' Definition of *Droit*," in accordance with which
one is in the presence of a juridical situation when the following conditions
are fulfilled:

1. When there are two distinct beings, A and B, each of which can be either a
   physical person or a moral person (individual, collective, or abstract), and
   when there is an interaction between these two beings—that is, when A's
   action generates B's reaction, suppressing this action or tending to do so;
2. When there is an intervention, i.e., a voluntary act, of a third C, [who is]
   supposed to be able to be anyone at all (inside an exclusive group of a
   given Society at a given epoch); and finally,
3. When the interaction between A and B provokes every time that it recurs
   (by itself or by a solicitation coming from A, with or without B's consent)
   C's intervention, who irresistibly annuls (by his will, act, or goal) B's reaction (as will, act, or goal). (*Right*, 106)

From the lengthy discussions that lead from the first to the second definition,
I wish to discuss two crucial points about the intervenor C. In the first definition, Kojève refers to C as impartial and disinterested (acting thus, he must
be motivated by something other than interest, and this will ultimately turn
out to be something quite Kantian, a specific goal of willing to make justice
prevail). But in a merely external behaviorist way (from whose standpoint in-
trospection is considered ambiguous evidence), how can one know that C is
impartial or disinterested? Isn't everyone interested somehow? The existence
and importance of this problem, Kojève notes, underlie the fact that human
beings often look to God for true justice; *droit* is something that can only be
fully supported by something divine (viz., separated from the interests of this
spatial-temporal world, something eternal; we are reminded of the connection of the judge's authority to Eternity discussed in the previous section of
this chapter). Instead, therefore, of the unobservable and perhaps unattain-
able "disinterestedness," the alternative external substitute criterion can be
that the intervenor C can be anyone at all, with the notion that anyone at all
would intervene in the same way in accordance with some legal rule; this approach finds reflection in the practice of choosing judges or jurors by lot:

impartiality or disinterestedness means in external practice (since we cannot
see reliably into the hearts of men) that anyone at all, randomly chosen, can
appropriately intervene and do justice. But now another question arises: Is
the intervenor C really "anyone at all" in the universal abstract sense? In any
real system of justice, some are included, some are excluded. For instance,
some societies have excluded a whole class of slaves from an active share in
the system of justice; others excluded women; and so on. The actual system
of *droit* is enacted by the dominant forces in a given society; hence, for any
real, or positive, system of *droit*, the "anyone at all" who intervenes as C is
a member of an exclusive group of a particular society at a particular moment
of time. These qualifications to "anyone at all" are necessary to capture actual or real, positive right, whereas the first definition captured rather a rationalist formal ideal of right than the real practice of actual human societies.
If the society became *homogeneous*, however, these qualifications would no
longer be needed, given that no one would then be excluded; finally, then, the
purely rationalist definition of right would be realized and the qualifications,
needed to capture the various positive *droits* of different societies at varying
times, can be dropped. "In the universal and homogenous State, therefore, the
'rationalist' theory of *Droit* coincides with the 'historical or sociological' theory. That is the very core of Hegelianism, or, if one prefers, of the dialectical
understanding of history" (*Right*, 92).

But will that State, or Empire, come to pass? Kojève states once again here
his position that one cannot now know: "As long as the Empire will not be realized, *Droit* will remain relative. And it is very possible that this empire will
never be realized; for historical evolution proceeds by negation—that is,
freely, or in an unforeseeable way" (*Right*, 92).

The other crucial point to discuss, in order fully to grasp Kojève's conception, is the notion of C's action. Human action, according to Kojève, involves
three phases: will or intention, act, and goal. The C who intervenes to assure
A's right against B's reaction that would impede it may intervene at any or all
of these three phases. By announcing and promulgating the legal rule, C aims
at preventing B from having the will to react against A (and this intervention
will be successful to the extent that B respects the law's authority). In this
mode, C acts as legislator who lays down and promulgates rules of right. Or
C may act to stop B's action, as judge proper, through his judgment that effectively orders B not to react. Or, finally, B may in fact have reacted against
A's right, and in this case C acts to remedy A's violated right and to annul the
goal that B sought to attain through that violation (here we have the realms of
rectification and punishment or retribution). In short, the juridical intervenor
C can be legislator, judge, or judicial police. Kojève underlines that the juridical legislator is doing something fundamentally different from legislators

who act to advance the State's interest, often calling the product of their work *law*; *raison d'état* and *droit* are different things. Accordingly, he suggests, there might be a case to be made for separating judicial legislation from the political legislature.

Our basic conception of right involves the notion that the specifically juridical actor, C, prevails in his intervention to support A's right against B's actual or potential opposition. This is reflected in the second definition's statement that C's intervention "irresistibly" annuls B's reaction. Our concept of right is not simply the notion of a certain set of opinions; real right must be supported by a sanction. In practice this means that the enforcement of right must be supported by the full force of the state. Now in actual societies so far, of course, this ideal is always only partially, that is, more or less fully, attained. In every society there is some real possibility that B's reaction may not in fact be annulled—for instance, if B successfully flees to another jurisdiction. But if the final goal of historical development is a *universal* empire, this shortcoming in real right could be overcome. (In the meantime, of course, separate systems of right in separate sovereign states may make agreements, for instance regarding extradition, that help to move toward the ideal of irresistible enforcement.) Thus a final universal and homogeneous empire would fully realize (or actualize) right, and one can also say that the tendency of right to move toward its own fuller realization contributes to humanity's movement toward a universal and homogeneous state.

Why does C intervene? C's intervention, in principle disinterested or impartial, must be motivated by something: by the recognized existence of certain views of right. These views constitute a whole system of rights and related phenomena such as obligations; taken together, they constitute a conception of justice. For intervention on behalf of right to take place, there must be some human interest in justice as such. Justice itself, of course, is no less a disputed concept than any other human matter: in particular, the Hegelian Kojève of course finds that it has evolved throughout history; it is not a Platonic eternal idea but an emerging and varying human reality. *Droit*, however, presents itself as something eternal and unchanging—that is indeed an attribute of any system of right. In fact, societies move from one system of right to another, by way of revolution. The system of right does not so much evolve as get replaced with another system—and each system presents itself as fixed and rooted in eternal principles of justice. And there is a human possibility of acting for the sake of realizing justice, doing what is right, independently of other motivations.

The relationship of a system of right—involving a society's threefold "C": juridical legislator, judge proper, and judicial police—to the state is complex. For potential right to become actual or real, it must be supported by the state;

realized right is necessarily connected to the state, but the state and the political are themselves different from a system of right. Kojève follows Carl Schmitt in asserting that the fundamental political distinction is between friend and enemy. A state is a society of friends that defines itself as opposed to the others as enemies, actual or potential. When a state acts for a *raison d'état*, it is not acting juridically. The other key feature of the state is the distinction between governors and governed, and the state's relation to its citizens is also not juridical. Political laws, for instance, that define the state's relation to its citizens, are not juridical; there is no impartial C who can support right through intervention on the interaction of two parties A and B, because the state that must act as C is itself already the party B. (The "governors" are the "exclusive group" any one of whom can serve as C in accordance with Kojève's second behaviorist definition of *droit*.) In the limited case of a universal state, the political aspect of friends versus enemies would disappear. It is doubtless because this defining characteristic of a state would no longer exist that Kojève here often refers to humanity's end state as a universal and homogeneous *empire*. In this end state, the empire's actions would still involve the administration of justice, indeed this would be its most important task, but political *raisons d' état* would no longer apply. Until then, tension and conflict, on the one hand, and interdependence and mutual support, on the other, exist between the juridical system and the state, between justice and the political good at which reasons of state aim.

Right as such has its own specific character and autonomy. The attempt to reduce the whole juridical realm to economic interest loses sight of the distinctively juridical character of the impartial intervenor C. The economic dimension of life is, to be sure, distinctively human. Economic activity is not biological life; "the 'economic materialism' of Marxists is materialism in name only" (*Right*, 177). Marx tried to explain human life through distinctively human work, but he was wrong to drop the other part of the Hegelian anthropology: the desire for recognition and the fight for pure prestige. Work cannot be a source of *droit*:

> Work sets man against Nature. Now the relations between man and Nature have nothing juridical about them; for no human being can play the role of the "impartial and disinterested third" in this case. No one would seriously want to defend the interests of Nature against those of man, and in the case of a conflict between them, everyone will automatically side with man against Nature. (*Right*, 178)

A passionate contemporary environmentalist might wish to reject this formulation of Kojève's, but I believe it to be basically defensible: Nature is not a party to a judicial action; when people use laws and judicial process to defend Nature, they are in fact acting for the sake of an asserted rightful interest of society (a collective human person; A) in certain aspects of the natural environment against another party whose action would infringe on that right (B). While work cannot in Kojève's analysis be a source of *droit*, economic exchange is closely connected to the juridical phenomenon; indeed "in the vast majority of cases, the legal rules of modern *Droit* have in mind exchanges of an economic nature" (*Right*, 178).

The distinctive character of juridical action cannot be reduced to economics or to utilitarian happiness or to political reasons of state. Right, the juridical, the rules of just action, justice—these often overlap with religion and theological beliefs; certainly religion typically commands justice for the sake of the soul's salvation. But, Kojève argues, the authentic religious relation involves two persons, man and God, not the three persons of a juridical situation. Similarly, morality may command justice; but the realm of morality fundamentally involves one person's pursuit of the ideal of moral perfection (and morality may teach one not to judge others, whereas the juridical phenomenon is above all that of the impartial judge). Morality and justice often coincide, for instance in the command not to commit suicide; but justice may forbid it because of a rule of right that specifies what one owes to society, whereas morality may forbid it as falling short of one's ideal of individual perfection. A concrete human being is an economic man or woman, a citizen, a subject and object of *droit*, a moral man, and a religious man. The realm of concern and the distinctive motive of action of the just man, however, are specific and autonomous in relation to the other distinctively human phenomena.

Kojève's account of the origin and evolution of right and justice, part two of this volume, is an "application of fundamental principles of Hegel's phenomenological anthropology to the phenomenon of *Droit*, more exactly to the idea of Justice that constitutes its base" (*Right*, 206). Presupposing the interpretation of Hegel that he had published in his 1939 article, Kojève recapitulates the anthropogenetic struggle for recognition that issues in nascent humanity's bifurcation into master and slave. He makes clear that either taken simply is a kind of logical abstraction—the master is act without potential, the slave potential without act. Real humanity is their synthesis as citizen: "Man is therefore *real* only to the extent that he is a Citizen: the Master and the Slave are only logical 'principles,' which do not exist in fact in a pure state" (*Right*, 213). The stages of history are different ways in which elements of mastery and of slavery have been copresent in the human world.

Since humanity is understood here as arising through the original or anthropogenetic fight to the death for recognition, two types of right and justice emerge from this initial human situation. When one thinks of the world of masters and slaves, one is at first, of course, struck by its inequality. But the inequality between masters and slaves does not in itself involve a juridical principle; the realm of right and justice in the world dominated by masters arises in the masters' dealing with each other. And more primordially, the equal risk of life and the equally shared consent of (future) master and (future) slave to begin the fight founded the connections between justice and equality. The masters' justice or aristocratic justice is one of strict equality. Each master is identical and equal to every other master, for each has become human or manifested his humanity through persevering in the risk of life in the fight for recognition. Masters take their humanity as something that ought to exist, and they attribute its existence to their going all the way in the risk of their life in the fight for recognition. But since all such risk of life is identical to every other, the masters tend to see each other in their humanity as equal. From this fundamental origin and basis, then, the situation, rights, and status of all the masters are identical to each other, and the conception of right and justice that prevails in their world is one of strict equality. In consequence, the emphasis of their idea of justice, and their thinking about what ought to be, is on identity and status. Their principle of justice is hostile to inequality, and therefore not only to change but even to exchange. It is in accordance with this basic character of aristocratic justice that aristocracies may tend to make landed properties permanent and inalienable (as was the case in some Greek cities, and as Plato's Athenian Stranger recommends with some qualifications in *The Laws*).

By contrast, the justice that dominates the consciousness of slaves comes from their behavior in the original fight for recognition: each slave experienced deep fear at the possibility of the loss of life, and chose instead to submit to the master in order to find security for life. The slave exchanged autonomy for security, finding it acceptable to give up freedom with terror of death in exchange for security in slavery to the master. This initial act was the recognition of equivalence between risk of life with mastery and security with slavery. The world as seen by slaves is filled with inequalities, but starting from their original behavior, they discern equivalences between unequal beings. Accordingly, the slaves' notion of justice (and then bourgeois justice) is one not of strict equality or identity, but of equivalence, exchange, contract, recognition of difference, and the linking of the different through equivalences. A world dominated by such a view of justice is much more favorable to exchange, to commerce, and to social mobility.

Both conceptions of justice, according to Kojève, are ideal types, just as pure master and pure slave are. In real political societies, some elements of both the aristocratic justice of equality and the bourgeois justice of equivalence are present, rather in the same way that, according to Nietzsche's argument, all complex civilizations contain elements both of master morality and of slave morality blended together in various ways. History, in fact, moves toward a final synthesis of the masters' justice of equality and the slaves' justice of equivalence in the citizens' justice of equity, which Kojève sometimes calls the socialist conception of justice as equity.

The justice of the masters has a kind of completeness in itself; taking all juridical persons as strictly equal (and taking only masters as juridical persons, excluding slaves, women, children), this justice tends to stay in identity to itself. But eventually the observation of the humanity of the unequal impinges itself on social consciousness, and so the justice of equivalence held by the slaves comes to interact with the masters' justice of strict equality. This interaction, partial synthesis, and eventually complete synthesis of bourgeois justice with aristocratic justice produce the justice of the citizen or equity. Each type of justice modifies the other over time. Kojève illustrates this process through a clear example regarding the distribution of food for dinner. One might well begin with strict equality: it is just that all should get an equal share of food. But then one sees that some are hungrier than others, and one could modify this by moving toward a justice of equivalence, in accordance with which the amount of food distributed might be proportioned to need as manifested by hunger. But then the element of justice as equality might reassert itself, by leading one to inquire why some are hungrier than others. Let's say that it turns out that this difference comes from the fact that some have had no lunch; one might then proceed to try to eliminate this difference through implementing some new egalitarian measure that is perceived as right from the standpoint of justice as equality. Thus equivalence (which is a kind of equality, like Aristotle's proportional equality) and strict equality (like Aristotle's absolute or arithmetic equality) mutually affect each other, and human society evolves toward a balanced synthesis of the two. At the limit, they would be fully harmonized with each other (with equality prevailing except to the extent that irreducible difference requires the continuation of equivalences). This analysis of the historical evolution of justice combines in a coherent manner the idea of justice as absolute and eternal (justice as ultimate synthesis in the universal and homogeneous empire) with the human experiences that underlie the notion that justice is something ever-changing and relative to historical circumstances.

Part three of the book, just under one-half of the whole, deals with "The System of *Droit*." In it Kojève presents a systematic analysis of all the applications of the principle of justice in all the various distinguishable parts of *droit*: national and international, public, penal, private, and so on. His discussion looks toward the final synthesis of *droit* as it will be worked out in the universal and homogeneous empire at the end of history, but he frequently indicates that the precise details cannot be known in advance. For instance, in discussing the family law portion of private *droit*, he provides fascinating discussions about the character and function of the family: its fundamental basis of course is *la parenté* (kinship or blood relationship), that is, something that has to do with what one is as distinguished from what one does. The family satisfies the need to be loved for what one is (something different from being honored or recognized for what one does), and its chief activities are to educate the next generation and to propagate the family patrimony or heritage, in the broadest sense, forever into the future. Of course, we observe that the state has taken over much of the task of education, and we note as well that productive property can to a high degree be owned and managed by the state rather than in the traditional manner by families. Doubtless for these among other reasons, Kojève, while certain that all problems involving conflicts between familial and political *droit* will be resolved in the universal and homogeneous state, makes the following strong statement of uncertainty regarding the family: "The familial *Droit* of this State of the future is difficult to predict" (*Right*, 420n124).

Particularly significant and extensive is Kojève's discussion of the *droit* of economic society. He noted earlier that most of modern *droit* deals with commercial exchanges, property rights, and other economic matters. This is not, to be sure, a novel observation; Madison, for example, had already indicated in the famous Federalist No. 10 that the principal task of modern legislation was to regulate the conflicting economic interests of society. This topic is of particular interest as regards Kojève's thought, of course, because the issue of whether communism or capitalism would prevail as the future of mankind in the years ahead loomed large in the mid-twentieth century, and Kojève appears to consider it at this time as something of great importance, as he continued to do in 1946 when he wrote that serious interpretation of Hegelianism involved the question of whether Marxism or some other form of social and economic organization was going to win out as the program for humanity's future. As in his seminar on Hegel, Kojève here too decidedly favors communism or at least socialism. He often refers to the final synthesis, the justice of the citizen as a synthesis of aristocratic justice and bourgeois justice, as the *socialist* justice of equity.

We must remember, of course, that Kojève does not agree with any attempt to reduce all of human life to the economic dimension. That said, it remains the case that the economic dimension of life is, in his view, distinctively human and a major part of what human life is all about: the technological mastery of nature, made possible by the exchanges among human beings, through which a distinctively human world is created within the larger framework of the natural order. That economic life is distinctively human is a well-worn observation. Adam Smith, for instance, points out that human beings have a tendency to exchange things, to "truck and barter," in a way that no other animals display; this practice of exchanging things is a necessary condition for the development of the division of labor and specialization that make progress in production possible. Kojève, of course, presents a distinctively Kojèvean-Hegelian explanation of the source of this distinctively human economic behavior. Animals desire things, and in the presence of the natural object of desire they consume it. Humans, because of their originating as master and slave in the fight motivated by the desire for the nonnatural goal of recognition, become separated from and so take a distance on the immediate consumption of desired objects. The master's interaction with desired objects is mediated by the slave's work. More importantly for subsequent economic developments, the slave must work for the master and therefore works to prepare or create desired objects that he will not himself enjoy. The slave thus learns to separate himself from and so to take a distance on the objects of desire. Indeed, this stance toward the objects of desire becomes a deeply rooted habit. He thus becomes in some sense free in relation to those objects, free enough to conceive of a variety of uses for them other than immediate consumption—most importantly, the possibility of exchanging one thing for another. Correspondingly, the original and basic idea of justice that arises on the side of the slave, the justice of equivalence, is precisely the notion of justice that befits and promotes exchange.

Property from the standpoint of aristocratic justice is property in the most absolutely personal sense; it belongs to a person as his own, attached to him, fully and distinctively his. Property that is most fully one's own tends not to be alienable or exchangeable. From the standpoint of the bourgeois justice of equivalence, property is indeed one's own, but in a more qualified sense that admits of alienation and exchange. Accordingly, the historical developments in the realm of economics (work, division of labor, technique, exchange, modes of organizing all the preceding) come from the side of bourgeois justice. In the final synthesis, it is not clear how much will be socialized rather than left to private ownership. At the limit, if there were no personal or private property at all, no realm of economic *droit* would any longer exist. But would everything thus be removed from private ownership? Evoking human freedom, Kojève once again indicates that the future in this regard is unknowable; he argues, however, that the ultimate privacy of each human being's body (the limit to communism even in Plato's *Republic*; see 464D) is a basis for expecting that some economic *droit*, which necessarily involves private ownership, will remain even in the presumably socialist end state in which the modes of production and distribution would be fully controlled by the state.

Kojève's discussion of international *droit*, existing at the same time as the *droits* of many sovereign nations, is of particular interest, not least in our present circumstances. To understand the development of *droit* in general, and the relation of international and national *droits* in particular, one needs to distinguish between *droit* in actuality and *droit* in potentiality. The former exists as actually enforced, in principle irresistibly. The latter is an awareness of right and justice that may be enforced, but whose enforcement is somehow optional or in other ways less than fully reliable and irresistible. To take a simple example: in primitive enough circumstances, the revenge taken for a murder by the family of the murdered person is not juridical at all (there is no impartial intervenor C). With time, murder becomes a juridical affair and is dealt with as a matter of private or civil *droit*: the family of the murdered appeals to a judicial authority to pass judgment that awards damages and imposes some other sanction. Eventually, murder becomes a matter of public or penal *droit*: the murder is seen as an offense by the person B against that collective person, society, which is the injured party A; the judicial power, C, intervenes on its own initiative to do justice between them. *Droit* becomes pretty much fully actualized or realized when the judicial function is carried out by the State, which intervenes now irresistibly. On the way toward this full actualization, the *droit* in question exists in potentiality, and only partly in actuality.

This distinction enables one to discuss more fully how international *droit* comes into being and develops. The most fully actualized *droits* are those of sovereign national states. But transnational societies—economic, scientific, religious, and other—exist as well. These societies may recognize principles of right, which at that stage exist chiefly in potentiality. But to the extent that the principles in question are in fact acted upon in the same way by the several national judicial systems, the international principles of right begin to move from mere existence in potentiality into realization. This movement can lead to the creation of institutions directed to achieving fuller actualization of that international *droit*; eventually some kind of federation may exist to actualize right in some dimension, and at the limit might come the universal and homogeneous empire. This line of thinking about *droit* brings forth a very interesting suggestion about how different national systems could be harmonized peacefully, as they come gradually to recognize each other's legitimacy in ever-expanding areas of law, and how in this way movement could take place toward a universal system of law. A universal and homogeneous empire could come about from one state's (or empire's) succeeding in universal conquest. But Kojève also lets us see the possibilities of gradual peaceful evolution toward federations that embrace and, in regard to the system of *droit*, eventually supersede the several *droits* of sovereign nations. Kojève's later practical work on the European Union, it seems, could well be understood as his attempt to actualize this possibility.

EMPIRE

Kojève's "Latin Empire: Sketch of a Doctrine of French Policy" looked at the world in August 1945. Whereas in *La Notion de l'Autorité* he had broached the possibility of a national-revolutionary project for France and in the *Phenomenology of Right* he had spoken about national systems of right that might eventually give way to something larger, here he definitely announced the actual end of the nation-state as the dominant political form in the world. Germany was the decisive test case, of a particularly large, highly developed, and disciplined nation-state that engaged in a war for nationalist purposes. This effort was anachronistic: it was defeated because a nation-state can no longer provide what is needed for all-out war with the most recently developed technologies. The decisive criterion of political efficacity is autonomous will or the will to autonomy, which depends on the real capacity to make war; and now only a political entity larger than the nation-state can successfully carry through war on the largest scale. This political entity that is larger than a nation-state Kojève calls Empire.

In Kojève's view, the world in 1945 had not yet come to the realistic possibility of a political entity that would embrace all of humanity. A universal and homogeneous state, a political entity for all of humanity, still lay in the future. Indeed, it was the "political genius" of Stalin to recognize that, while the era of the nation-state was over, the Trotskyite "political orientation toward humanity" as a whole was still utopian. The *national* socialism of Hitler was anachronistic; the socialist *internationalism* of Trotsky was utopian, as was liberal-pacifist (and therefore administrative rather than political) internationalism; the political form of the present (1945) was the Empire, for example, Stalin's Slavo-Soviet Empire. It was not only Stalin who recognized this crucial political fact. In Kojève's judgment, it was likewise through "the comprehension of *imperial* reality that the directors of the British state, notably Churchill," similarly manifested "political genius" ("Empire," 94–95).

It is in the context of this short political essay of 1945, I think, that one can best understand a position stated by Kojève that Raymond Aron found most disturbing. I refer, of course, to Kojève's notorious description of himself as a *stalinien de strict observance* (a strictly observant Stalinist) or as *la conscience de Staline* (the consciousness of Stalin, or better, the coming to consciousness of Stalin). Aron described himself as deeply puzzled and troubled by this shocking utterance, which Kojève did not make in ignorance of dreadful things that were taking place in the Soviet Union. Can Kojève really have been serious? Was it some strange residuum of Russian patriotism (Aron 1990, 66)? Or was it a some kind of gesture, of which many French intellectuals for over a century have been perhaps inordinately fond, to *épater les bourgeois* (shock the bourgeois)? Former Prime Minister Raymond Barre, in a fascinating interview with Dominique Auffret, suggested that Kojève's calling himself *la conscience de Staline* took place in an intellectual context of Marxist effervescence that Kojève found futile and a bit ridiculous. The phrase was also, Barre suggested:

> A type of provocation, of saying that he understood Marx better than the trademarked Marxist intellectuals, and above all that his understanding of Marx had not prevented him from moving on to practice where he found himself acting, in the ministry of national Economy. (Auffret, 420)

I would suggest that Kojève's phrase has two meanings, one very general and fundamental to his political philosophy, the other more specific to the politics of the mid-twentieth century. Insofar as he was a Marxist kind of Hegelian, Kojève was still looking toward the end of history as something yet to develop; in this regard, he viewed the communist or socialist project as the present working out of that future end and approved of Stalin as in fact doing the most impressive work, as leader of the Soviet Union, to bring that future to pass. On the other hand, Kojève saw the end state—the universal and homogeneous empire—as still distant. Though the era of nation-states was finally over with the defeat of Germany, the era in which universal humanity would be the relevant political body still was far enough away that action in its name remained utopian (that is, we did not yet have adequate political knowledge of the concrete real steps that would lead to it). The era before us was that of empires; Stalin with his "socialism in one country" (which is in effect, Kojève asserts here in "Empire," imperial socialism or socialist empire) was correct, as against the utopian internationalism of Trotsky (as well as against the national socialism of Hitler). In that way, Stalin had displayed "political genius," on the left (as Churchill and other British leaders had done, Kojève indicates with remarkable openness, on the right). Kojève himself, of course, was unquestionably a man of the left; but the complexity of his position found expression in his being described as a "Marxist of the right" (and being attacked as such, or more precisely as a fascist, in the East German press after a German translation of his *Introduction* appeared in 1958).

Kojève identified two empires then on the scene: the Anglo-American Empire and the Soviet-Slavic Empire. He anticipated that defeated Germany would likely adhere rather to the Anglo-American than to the Soviet Empire. France accordingly faced two grave dangers of destruction. First, the longer-range danger: it could be crushed by a possible future war between these two empires. Second, the more immediate threat: it might simply be dominated by a Germano-Anglo-American Empire. To avoid these two dire outcomes, Kojève sketched the possibility of France's taking the lead in a newly emerging empire, which he suggested could emerge on a Latin or Mediterranean basis (France, Spain, Italy, and their North African colonies, including, he ventured to hope, Italy's; he expresses the hope that France could urge the Allies to permit Italy's recovery of her lost North African colonies). This empire could stand between the Anglo-American and the Slavo-Soviet empires in more than a geographical sense alone. It might, Kojève suggested, find a middle way between the two in terms of economic and social order:

> For nothing proves that the "liberalism" based on great autonomous trusts and on the massive unemployment dear to the Anglo-Saxon block and the leveling and somewhat "barbarous" "statism" of the Soviet Union exhaust all the possibilities of rational economic and social organization. ("Empire," 107)

Kojève considers a political basis necessary for the long-term preservation of any civilization. Since France as a political entity of the first rank is no longer a real possibility, the preservation of French culture, of Latin culture, and really of Western culture as we know it in its full complexity and range must depend on the viability of a corresponding political entity. In accordance with this analysis, the greatest benefit of a Latin Empire would be the preservation of Latin, preeminently French, civilization (and those aspects of Western civilization of Latin provenance and character). Kojève describes this civilization, in contrast to the Anglo-Saxon and Slavo-Soviet, as "amortissante, pacifique, synthétique" (calming, peaceful, synthetic) ("Empire," 97). He describes it as endowed with a distinctive mentality characterized by "that art of leisure activities which is the source of art in general, by the aptitude to create that *'douceur de vivre'* which has nothing to do with material comfort, even by that *'dolce far niente'* which degenerates into simple laziness only if it does not come after a productive and fertile work." To this mentality he connects "a profound sense of beauty generally associated . . . with a very marked feeling for *la juste mesure*, and which permits the transformation of simple bourgeois well-being into aristocratic *'douceur de vivre.'*" This Latin mentality would not only be a basis for imperial union but would justify that empire before the world and history. Indeed, looking forward to the eventual definitive elimination of all national and social conflicts—"which is perhaps less far off than one thinks"—Kojève asserts that "one must admit that it is precisely to the organization and humanization of its leisure activities that future humanity will have to devote its efforts" ("Empire," 104). Reinforcing this idea, Kojève suggests that the Roman Catholic character (however secularized) of the Latin realm involves an abiding effort, with frequent recourse to art, "to organize and humanize the 'contemplative' or inactive life of man," whereas "Protestantism, hostile to the methods of artistic pedagogy, has above all been preoccupied with man as worker" ("Empire," 105).

These themes of culture, civilization, art, leisure, may seem surprising in the context of the sketch that examines political and imperial realities with a view to a long-term grand strategy. But as Kojève reminds us, Marx too—in this respect following Aristotle without necessarily realizing it—considered that "the final goal of progress, and therefore of socialism, is the desire to assure man a maximum of leisure" ("Empire," 104). And in that case, it seems reasonable to attribute high importance, or rather the highest importance, to the kind of activities to which that leisure is to be devoted. Kojève's cultural and artistic emphasis here is linked with the marked distaste for America and the emphatic aestheticism or fondness for formalism connected with Japan that he evinced later in his note to the second edition of *Introduction to the Reading of Hegel*. Thus we see that he reflected in concrete detail on all the qualities of the way of life that will emerge at the end of history, so that even in this most political of his essays, he sought the way to preserve what was most appealing about France in particular and Latin culture or civilization in particular.

The Latin Empire envisaged by Kojève would seek, as its chief or even sole goal of foreign policy, predominance over the Mediterranean Sea. This goal would bear a striking similarity, as he notes, to the ancient Romans' making of that sea into *mare nostrum*. Someone might say, he recognizes, that this slogan "has already been inscribed on the Fascists' standards, which were anything but glorious." Kojève, however, emphasizes that what was grotesque was not the goal itself, but the ridiculous Italian Fascist pretension to achieve it on the basis of a single nation; in contrast, he is proposing it as an imperial goal. Kojève's essay seems a bit out of date in some respects, in its inordinate fear of British influence and, most notably, in its continued acceptance of European colonialism. (But even in this latter respect he makes a remarkably interesting comment, to the effect that a Latin Empire might be able to work out the difficulties of many centuries' standing that afflict the relationship between Christian Europe and the Islamic world.) In most respects, the article is impressively prescient. In the event, of course, it was not a Latin Empire but rather the European Union (including Germany) that was to emerge in between the Anglo-American Empire and that of the Soviet Union. The complication of British membership in that European Union, opposed by Kojève and by De Gaulle, came to pass only after Kojève's death.

In discussing Kojève's remarks on the authority of the father (and of tradition, the past, etc.) in his monograph on authority, I noted his silence on what this authority—if reestablished as part of a complete political authority in modern times—would be involved in doing. His remarks about the cultural qualities of the Latin Empire suggest a fuller answer: the whole way of life, the cultural traditions, the spirit of a nation (or of a larger group of affiliated nations) might be the arena in which this power of the father would be at work to preserve traditions as links to the past, to keep them vital in the present, and to transmit them in a flourishing state to the future.

NOTES

1. Alexandre Kojève, *La notion de l'autorité*, ed. François Terré (Paris: Éditions Gallimard, 2004).

2. Alexandre Kojève, *Esquisse d'une phénoménologie du Droit: Exposé provisoire* (Paris: Éditions Gallimard, 1981); *Outline of a Phenomenology of Right*, ed. and trans. Bryan-Paul Frost and Robert Howse (Lanham, MD: Rowman & Littlefield, 2000).

3. An English translation by Erik de Vries, "Outline of a Doctrine of French Policy (August 27, 1945)" has appeared in the journal *Policy Review*, no. 126 (available at http://www.policyreview.org/aug04/kojeve_print.html). It includes some detailed political and economic analyses omitted from the version published by *La Règle du Jeu*.

4. Published in the January 15, 1939, issue of *Mesures* (fifth year, no. 1, 108 ff.) and used as the introduction or first chapter of *Introduction*; it is discussed in chapter 2.

5. For a fuller discussion of Kojève's analysis of the structure of human, historical time in comparison with biological and physical times, see chapter 2, pp. 38–39.

Chapter Four

The End of History:
In the Future or in 1806,
Communist or Capitalist?

By a remarkable chance, Kojève, who very rarely gave interviews (or, for that matter, public lectures), was interviewed by Gilles Lapouge shortly before his death; the interview was published in the *Quinzaine Littéraire* of July 1–15, 1968, soon after his death. In the interview, Kojève briefly sketches the most fundamental lines of his intellectual development. He tells of how, in reading Hegel's *Phenomenology of Spirit*, he at first thought that the notion of an end of history was more or less nonsense, "une billevesée" ("a silly tale"); eventually, however, when he had come to understand the *Phenomenology*, he came to see this idea of the end of history as a philosophical insight of genius. Of course, as he tells it, at that time he thought that Hegel was off by 150 years: the end of history was not Napoleon's universal empire as understood by Hegel, but the achievement of Stalin as understood by Kojève—even though, as he commented, he did not have the advantage of seeing Stalin ride by on horseback under his window;—"mais enfin" ("but—oh well"). This was Kojève's position regarding the historical status of the present when he taught his famous course on the *Phenomenology*; he held to this view in writing about authority and right during the war; and it was still his view in 1946, when he added footnotes to the forthcoming *Introduction à la Lecture de Hegel*, the book put together by the novelist Raymond Queneau consisting of notes and transcripts from Kojève's seminar from 1933–1939 (discussed in chapter 2).

Later on, after the Second World War (perhaps as early as 1948, according to the footnote that Kojève added to the second edition of *Introduction*), he changed his mind in one important respect: he came to understand, or at least to believe, that Hegel had gotten it right in the first place: history did in fact end in 1806. We can thus divide Kojève's mature intellectual life into two periods, which I shall simply call the earlier and the later: an earlier one in which, like Marx, he believed that the end of history had not yet been attained but was clearly visible in its essential outlines; and a later one in which he believed that the end of history had basically been attained in the Napoleonic aftermath of the French Revolution and that so-called world history since then has been the working out of less than world-historically fundamental details. In this chapter I endeavor to set forth and to understand the position taken by the later Kojève. What does it mean to say that history is in fact already over, and what implications does that assertion or belief have for one's view of present and future human life?

Kojève restates his early stance toward Hegelian thought in its relation to the end of history with clarity and vigor in the following statement near the end of his article "Hegel, Marx, and Christianity," published in 1946.

> If there has been from the beginning a Hegelian left and right, this is also *all* that there has been since Hegel. For if one abstracts from the remnants of the past which Hegel knew and described ("liberalism" included) . . . one observes that there has been strictly nothing outside of Hegelianism (whether conscious or not), whether on the plane of historical reality itself, or on that of such thought or discourse as has had historical repercussions.
>
> In our time, as in the time of Marx, Hegelian philosophy is not a truth in the proper sense of the term: it is less the adequate discursive revelation of a reality, than an idea or an ideal, that is to say, a "project" which is to be realized, and therefore proved true, through action. . . .
>
> One can therefore say that, for the moment, every interpretation of Hegel, if it is more than idle talk, is nothing but a program of struggle and one of work (and one of these "programs" is called *Marxism*). And this means that the work of an interpreter of Hegel takes on the meaning of a work of political propaganda. . . . It may be that, in fact, the future of the world, and therefore the meaning of the present and the significance of the past, depend, in the final analysis, on the way in which the Hegelian writings are interpreted today.

Kojève's use of the term "propaganda" is striking, and suggests of course that his own interpretation of Hegel had a propagandistic meaning. In fact, he explicitly said as much about his course in the letter to Tran-Duc-Thao. I quoted part of that letter near the beginning of chapter 3, and the passage continues as follows: "My course was essentially a work of propaganda destined to strike people's minds (*frapper les esprits*). That is why I consciously reinforced the role of the dialectic of Master and Slave and, in a general way, schematized the contents of the phenomenology" (Jarcyk and Labarrière, 64). How should we think of this "work of political propaganda"? Certainly it goes along with the notion of the end of history as not yet a truth but a reasonable project (or rather, the only rationally defensible project). With such a view, why should one not want to promote the realization of this decisive historical step forward in any way one can, which for a philosopher might most obviously involve ideological or propagandistic work?[1] More particularly, Kojève took the view that the future, as the product of human freedom and hence as contingent, could belong to either right-wing or left-wing Hegelians. The development of fascist ideology contained substantial Hegelian elements,[2] and the National Socialists too were Hegelian in at least some aspects, certainly including their glorification of the state, their rejection of liberalism, and their sense of historical mission. Kojève rejected these positions as anachronistic, as misinterpretations of isolated parts of the Hegelian understanding. By contrast, it is clear, Kojève considered that his own interpretation of Hegel, presented from 1933, the year of Hitler's coming to power, to 1939, just before the outbreak of war, would help to promote the left-wing project of correctly understood Hegelianism over other possible variants, doubtless most importantly those of the Fascists and Nazis.

The fullest account of Kojève's change of mind on this crucial matter of the end of history is to be found in the footnote added to the second edition of his *Introduction to the Reading of Hegel*, published in 1962. The importance of this issue for him is exhibited by the fact that this was the only addition that Kojève chose to make to the book on this occasion of a second edition. He begins by criticizing his position stated in his text (from 1938 to 1939) and his footnote in the first edition (added in 1946): these do not, he now asserts, adequately address the question of the continuation of humanity, the maintenance of human activities, after the end of history. There he had said that at the end of history man remains alive as animal while Man properly so-called (action negating the given, etc.) disappears, but that "all the rest can be preserved indefinitely: art, love, play, etc." (159). Now he asserts that if man becomes an animal again, his activities will no longer remain specifically human but will be similar to those of animals (birds building nests, cicadas singing, and so on). He suggests too that genuine discourse, as distinguished from the so-called languages of bees and ants, might disappear, and the human altogether would return to animality.

He claims that man's return to animality seemed to him a not unthinkable possibility in 1946, but that by 1948 he had come to understand that Hegel had been more completely correct than he used to think:

> I understood that the Hegelian-Marxist end of History was not yet to come, but was already a present, here and now. Observing what was taking place around me and reflecting on what had taken place in the world since the Battle of Jena, I understood that Hegel was right to see in this battle the end of History properly so-called. In and by this battle the vanguard of humanity virtually attained the limit and the aim, that is, the *end*, of Man's historical evolution. (160)

He draws out the necessary inference that "from the authentically historical point of view, the two world wars with their retinue of large and small revolutions had only the effect of bringing the backward civilizations of the peripheral provinces into line with the most advanced (real or virtual) European historical positions." Moreover, he goes on to assert that the elimination of anachronistic vestiges is

> more advanced in the North American extensions of Europe than in Europe itself. One can even say that, from a certain point of view, the United States has already attained the final stage of Marxist "communism," seeing that, practically, all the members of a "classless society" can from now on appropriate for themselves everything that seems good to them, without thereby working any more than their heart dictates. (160–161)

He saw that the Sino-Soviets were moving toward the same goal as the Americans, inferred that the "American way of life" looked like "the 'eternal present' future of all humanity," and concluded that "Man's return to animality appeared no longer as a possibility that was yet to come, but as a certainty that was already present." But then a voyage (1959) to Japan led him to consider the possibility that snobbery, formalized values empty of content in the historical human sense, could provide the basis for the continued existence of humanity in the posthistorical future; and so to ask whether the West might be Japonized rather than Japan's being Westernized.

This remarkable note invites several comments. First of all: his characterization of America is an extreme of provocative overstatement or bold extrapolation. Certainly the majority of Americans now, and doubtless an even greater majority in 1962, would be surprised to learn that they can have whatever they want without working any more than they please. Here Kojève seems to exaggerate outrageously. But why? What point is conveyed, what purpose is served, by such overstatement? The easiest answer, and perhaps the truest as well, is that strongly paradoxical formulations of this sort seek to provoke thought. Perhaps too, Kojève was expressing here a point of view that has been taken over the years by many philosophers and other intellectuals, from Socrates, Diogenes the Cynic, and Epicureans among the ancients to Rousseau, Marx, and John Stuart Mill among the moderns: if people are able to have all the things that the philosopher in question considers enough for them (meeting their real needs and providing all the genuine satisfactions of which they are in fact capable), these people must properly be understood to have all that they want (or at least can reasonably want). It was on the basis of such an understanding that John Stuart Mill argued (in *Principles of Political Economy* Book IV, chapter VI) that an eventual stationary state in the economy might provide greater satisfactions in life than we now enjoy from our continual efforts to keep things forever growing; and similarly, Marx relied on the notion of a definitive overcoming not only of necessity but presumably also of scarcity as well in order to make believable to himself the whole conception of a realm of freedom.

What seems inadequate about this point of view, if indeed this is the view that Kojève has taken here, is its assumption that human ingenuity (science, technology, economy) has definitively overcome nature to such a degree as to supply all human wants, for certainly from the standpoint of commonsense understanding, we seem to be as far away from any such condition as a typical hardworking American of today feels from being able to have whatever he wants without working any more than his heart dictates. And also, as I noted toward the end of chapter 1, although Kojève asserts the completion of philosophical development, he seems altogether open to the idea that physics will continue to develop without any known limit or goal. Furthermore, one wonders whether human beings are not such as always,[3] regardless of how much abundance of various existing goods is available to them, to be searching for something better. If so, it makes sense to ask whether human dominion over nature could ever be complete, or whether the human being might always tend to seek novel satisfactions (including more complete knowledge in the domain, for example, of physics). And if that is the case, might not this human trait provide support for the continued existence of distinctively human life rather than the relapse into animality that Kojève contemplates here?

Kojève seems to be no less bold, perhaps even bolder, in asserting that the Sino-Soviets are simply headed in the same direction as the Americans,[4] although I would certainly say today that this particular assertion appears to have been better confirmed by subsequent events than his description of or prediction about American life has been. In this regard, of course, he asserts a thoroughgoing convergence theory regarding what were then commonly called the East and the West; I discuss the key economic aspect of that view a bit later in this chapter in connection with his lecture on colonialism.

Most puzzling of all, surely, is Kojève's discussion of Japanese allegedly posthistorical life and its formalism or snobbery. In the interview with Gilles Lapouge in 1968 Kojève still maintained this view of Japan; he put it strongly and colorfully in these terms:

Consider Japan: there's a country that deliberately protected itself from history during three centuries; it put a barrier between history and itself, so well that it perhaps permits us to foresee our own future. And it's true that Japan is an astonishing country. An example: snobbery, by its nature, is the purview of a small minority. Now, what Japan teaches us, is that one can democratize snobbery. Japan is eighty million snobs. Next to the Japanese people, English high society is a bunch of drunken sailors.

It is hard to know whether this kind of formalism that Kojève discusses in connection with Japan is really a serious candidate to be the permanent support for our posthistorical humanity. It is baffling to me why, if there truly is a risk (or even, as he seems to say in regard to America, a present certainty) of man's return to animality, Kojève would not pursue the issue in more detail and depth. Let us grant that the Japanese display snobbery to a high degree, but is that really something sufficiently different from more or less similar behaviors in others, the French, say, or even the Americans, to produce the difference between preserving humanity and lapsing into animality? Why does he not discuss other possibilities, such as education, which he elsewhere characterizes as the distinctive task of the human family and as a distinctively human process of negating the animal givens of nature as one forms new genuinely human beings? Perhaps philosophy is over if, in the decisive respect, Hegel was right and wisdom is now available; but for each real person, it is available only with the greatest difficulty. Would not all the learning that human beings must experience in order to grasp Hegelian wisdom continue to support the existence of our humanity more plausibly than arts of flower arrangement, tea ceremonies, and Noh theatre? Would not the philosophical study of history, reviewing in one's mind all the negations in action and in thought that have taken place in human history on the way to its fulfillment, suffice to keep alive the understanding remembrance and thus the continued actuality of distinctively human being? But perhaps Kojève's puzzling statement, with its striking brevity and remarkable omissions, is meant precisely to provoke questions like these, and so to kindle in readers a sense of the need to explore these possibilities further.[5]

That Kojève's statement here is chiefly meant as a provocation emerges from the following reflection as well. He speaks here as though "Japan" and "United States" were two ideal types, opposed to each other, tending to produce respectively either continued humanity on the basis of snobbery and formal aestheticism or a return to animality. Regarding the latter, I suppose that he has in mind traits of the "American way of life" that have provoked keen comments from observers at least as early as Tocqueville: a preference for fast and easy satisfactions, a kind of informality or even formlessness of life, an impatience with tradition, a practical utilitarianism combined with something like contempt for theory and contemplation, and so on. Now, ideal types do not exist actually in their purity, and for that reason Kojève pointed out, for example, that actual authorities are usually some kind of mixture of two or more of his four pure types of authority; and similarly, to give another example, he argued that the *droit* (right, law, juridical system) of master and of slave do not exist purely but in combinations of varying proportion. So here too, in my judgment, one should not think that Kojève seriously contemplates a strict dichotomy in reality between formalism and animality, but rather that, in the context of seeking to provoke thought, he sketches two ideal types to which he gives the names "Japan" on the one hand and "United States of America" or "the West" on the other.

However that may be, the problems left unresolved in this ironical and provocative note are, I believe, the chief reasons for the later Kojève's reputation as, finally, no longer a Hegelian systematic rationalist but some sort of postmodern ironist. I shall present a further reflection on that possible interpretation in the concluding chapter.

Although the matter under discussion here—the character of life at the end of history and the possible power of aesthetic formalism and perhaps other cultural traits and artifacts to sustain the distinctively human—is an issue confronted more fully and openly by the later Kojève than by the earlier, it is worth recalling that some of his earlier writings foreshadowed this high valuation of aesthetic formalism, although he did not earlier go so far as to suggest that it might provide the crucial support for humanity's continuation. In the proposal regarding a "Latin Empire," Kojève displayed a passionate attachment to preserving the fundamental elements of French and Latin culture and civilization from being overwhelmed by the Anglo-Saxon or Soviet alternatives. The importance that he attributed there to leisure, art, the style and rhythm of living, and even *dolce far niente* and aristocratic *douceur de vivre* loomed surprisingly large in his projected policy doctrine; and of course he contrasted these aspects of Latin life favorably with Anglo-American traits such as excessively liberal political economy accompanied by great "trusts" and high unemployment as well as with the excessive leveling and occasional barbarism of Slavo-Soviet life, going so far as to suggest that these aspects of Latin civilization would justify the project of a Latin empire by serving "the cultural interests of all of humanity." And an article on Kandinsky in 1936, "Les peintures concrètes de Kandinsky" ("The concrete paintings of Kandinsky"), displays Kojève as having given considerable thought to another aesthetic question, what the final historical outcome of the development of plastic art would be.

In the 1950s, Kojève wrote two critical essays on contemporary novels; both deal with the character of life in the posthistorical epoch. The first and longer of these, entitled "Les Romans de la Sagesse" ("Novels of Wisdom"), deals with three novels by his friend Raymond Queneau: *Pierrot Mon Ami* (*My Friend Pierrot*), *Loin de Rueil* (*Far from Rueil*; a published English translation uses the title *The Skin of Dreams*), and *Le Dimanche de la Vie* (*The Sunday of Life*). Kojève describes the main characters in these novels as exhibiting life at the end of history; rather ironically, it seems, he describes them as philosophers who have attained the object of their search, or more precisely, as posthistorical wise men. The irony is that they are in no way evidently wise in any usual sense: they are not particularly learned or educated; they are not scholars or intellectuals. But, according to Kojève, Queneau depicts them as living in accordance with a kind of posthistorical wisdom. For instance, Pierrot works at an amusement park in Paris, in a funhouse where gusts of air lift the skirts of female visitors, to the delight of a bunch of onlookers whom the funhouse staff call *philosophes*—philosophers. (They are also *voyous*, slang for something like hoodlums or bums, but the word *voyou* is etymologically related to the word *voie*, street, and thus suggests their being street people— as were, of course, certain philosophers like Socrates or Diogenes.) Pierrot also takes a job transporting some trained animals from the south of France up to Paris; his interactions with these well-trained animals seem scarcely distinguishable from his dealings with other human beings. The ups and downs of life, the modest expectations, the equable disposition, the delight in simple pleasures of the moment, all these make Pierrot seem to exemplify something like the Stoic or Epicurean philosophic manner of living. The absence of human longings, of tragedy, of noble aspiration, could in itself make the reader think that the depiction updates the last men deplored by Nietzsche; but in fact the novel has a completely different tone and conveys an altogether different spirit: the character is truly engaging and sympathetic.

Barbara Wright, the English translator of *The Sunday of Life*, justly comments that most people have found it one of the sunniest and happiest of Queneau's novels. Certainly it is the book that is most evidently influenced by Queneau's serious study and close friendship with the Hegelian Kojève. *Le Dimanche de la Vie* takes its title from a passage in which Hegel discusses Dutch paintings of everyday life: ". . . it is the Sunday of life, which levels everything, and rejects everything bad; men gifted with such good humor cannot be fundamentally bad or base."[6] And the protagonist, Private Brû, "in general thought of nothing, but when he did, had a preference for the Battle of Jena," and toward the end of the story, he takes a vacation to see that famous battleground.

The second article, "Le dernier monde nouveau" ("The Last New World"), discusses Françoise Sagan's first two novels, *Bonjour Tristesse* (*Hello Sadness*) and *Un Certain Sourire* (*A Certain Smile*). The article's tone, though ironic like the first, is in other respects quite different, for in the first the irony seems friendly and respectful, in the second rather more biting. In particular, while praising her frank depiction, holding back nothing, of a world with no place for real manliness (courage, daring, and other warlike qualities), his irony seems rather heavy. He depicts her as finally making public and explicit what was first understood at the time of Napoleon by Beau Brummel and the Marquis de Sade: that no serious place remained for warlike valor, and consequently standing out from the crowd or winning distinction would have to be achieved in other ways. But in fact his ridicule is directed not so much at Françoise Sagan but at those who try, anachronistically now at the end of history, to continue to celebrate manly courage in our present circumstances. In particular, Ernest Hemingway, though not explicitly named, is referred to in order to illustrate the last desperate recourse of someone searching to celebrate manliness (perhaps, Kojève mischievously suggests, because of doubts on that score regarding himself): his search achieves its first result with his depiction of the great battle of man versus bull, and ultimately culminates in the epic struggle of man versus fish. The tone of Kojève's article conveys, on the one hand, something akin to a conservative lament for the lost possibility of realizing qualities of manliness in the world and a contemptuous perspective on certain features of the present (such as men becoming objects of physical attraction on the basis of smooth skin, attractive color, and the like, in ways that used to characterize women, rather than achieving desired status through manly, warlike deeds). On the other hand, the article's overall structure of rational argument suggests that the very sentiment regarding manliness and courage thus evoked is anachronistic, a kind of romantic longing for which no reasonable case can be made now.

A crucial aspect of Kojève's later thought on this matter of the end of history—the whole question of political economy—found expression in a rare public lecture, arranged by Carl Schmitt, that Kojève gave in 1957 in Düsseldorf. It is of particular interest since, dealing with economic matters, it conveys some of Kojève's views in the area in which he was active in the postwar period up to the time of his death. The lecture was entitled "Kolonialismus in europäischer Sicht" ("Colonialism from a European Point of View"), and it deals with the fundamental questions of political economy posed by the world situation. Accordingly, this lecture helps us to understand more fully how the later Kojève could assert that history was in fact already over. It lets us see how and why he moved away from thinking of a real contest between important alternatives (economic, ideological, and other) for the future of humanity, between left-wing Hegelianism (Marxism) and the Western liberal societies, and toward asserting the convergence between Soviet communism and Western capitalism. It also presents us with the basic views about the present world situation, especially in its political-economic features, that doubtless underlie Kojève's practical work in the *Direction des relations économiques extérieures* of the French Ministry of Finance.

Kojève here claims that Marx was altogether correct in his analysis of the fundamental failing of the capitalist order: capitalism encouraged technological progress and increased productivity, but it failed to share the fruits of that progress with the majority of the (working) population; this situation is in the long run untenable. Or stated otherwise: the owners of the advanced means of production, a small minority, aided by their control of the power of the state and other aspects of the economic order, kept the surplus value created by ever more productive labor and invested it elsewhere without sharing it with the workers themselves. Up to this point, Marx was correct in his analysis of capitalism. He thought further, and here wrongly, that participants in the capitalist order could do nothing to remedy this problem; the structures of a capitalist political economy would force all the capitalists to keep going down this same path. They would not have the foresight to act otherwise, and if they tried, the existing structures would in any case effectively prevent them from doing so. Only violent revolution could change things, by breaking down the capitalist order and replacing it with the new communist order. Kojève notes that some of the intellectual defenders of capitalism, certain kinds of free market economists, argued that no interference with market freedoms, such as unlimited freedom of contract, should be permitted. They did so with a view to defending capitalist free market society, but with a different intention they in fact agreed with Marx's error, namely in their belief that free market capitalism could not be peacefully changed for the better.

Other capitalists, however, came to understand the problem and tried, more practically, other approaches. They were mostly anonymous, but "one great ideologue" is known by name: Henry Ford. He aimed at making available a cheap automobile for a large public; he paid his workers more than the market wage required him to do, with a view to enabling them to be able to buy cars; he gave a large sum of money to the state of Massachusetts to build the first superhighway. And so Kojève calls Ford the one great authentic Marxist of the twentieth century, in that he acted to solve the problem of capitalism correctly diagnosed by Marx. Kojève quotes with approval a German saying: "Arme Kunden sind schlecte Kunden" ("Poor customers are bad customers"). Understanding this, Ford acted to raise the purchasing power of his workers; by Ford and many other practitioners, the capitalist political economy was thus reconstructed, by peaceful and democratic means, in a Marxist way (that is to say, toward a Marxist goal). And so the "social revolution," by being made unnecessary, was made impossible.

Other so-called Marxist theorists were for the most part romantics, who talked about economic systems different from what Marx himself had in view, while Ford was the true Marxist. His ideas eventually became systematized and put into forbidding economic jargon in a manner that obscured their fundamentally Fordist character, in the "full employment policies" that all the Western powers came to pursue. What Kojève calls "Fordist capitalism" solves the problem or contradiction of old-style capitalism in such a way as to promote the Marxist end of history. Socialism (not some ideal or other but the real system as exemplified by the Soviet Union) is like pre-Fordized old-style capitalism, except that the State rather than private capitalists invests the surplus value that is not shared with the workers. Let us note that this analysis shows the political-economic grounds for and the significance of the later Kojève's assertion that the United States is further advanced than the Union of Soviet Socialist Republics toward the Marxist end of history; in fact it is suggestive of more than just a minor difference of degree, in that he now describes Soviet state capitalism (my term, not his) in a way that shows it to be like nineteenth-century capitalism and so lagging a major stage behind modern Western capitalism. (Presumably when enough means of production have been accumulated, the Soviet Union could and would distribute more to the ordinary working class and so begin to catch up with the West in terms of income and standard of living.)

Now, this all sounds as though everything is fine and moving along smoothly toward the fuller working out of the end of history. Nowadays, however, as contrasted with the time of Marx himself (although predicted by Marx), the economy is not national, nor even Euro-American, but global. And looking at this global economy, Kojève indicates that, as colonialism, something like that old-style capitalism with its fundamental problem or contradiction still exists in the world. Colonialism is like old-style capitalism in a crucial respect: it takes surplus value away from the workers and invests it elsewhere. The difference is that old-style capitalism extracted surplus value and invested it as capital in the same country; colonialism extracts surplus value from other countries, underdeveloped or backward, of Asia and Africa and invests it back in the industrialized world. But the consequence is very similar: the Euro-American minority enjoys an ever-rising standard of living, while the Afro-Asian majority (Kojève omits mention here of South America for some reason) fails to share in the gains of increased productivity and is held down to a low level of income.

At the time of his lecture, then, Kojève sees the following kinds of political economic orders in the world. First: old-style capitalism as correctly analyzed by Marx no longer exists in the industrialized world, since capitalism has been rebuilt in a Fordist (or Marxist in a new sense) manner. Second: something like old-style capitalism still exists in the world under the name socialism or communism—not this or that ideal of socialism but the real order that actually exists in Soviet Russia, which is like old-style capitalism except in that the surplus value is held and invested by the state rather than by private firms and individuals. Kojève does not suggest what name should be used for the industrialized Western countries (he quite rightly does not appear to expect that the term "Fordist capitalism" will catch on). Probably some term like "social democracy" or "welfare state" would work for the time; eventually in Kojève's view the economic and political institutions of the end of history should emerge in full, in the eventual universal and homogeneous state that, as we have seen most clearly in "Latin Empire," still lies at some distance in the future but toward which both Western social democracy and Soviet (and Chinese) socialism are tending. Third: colonialism is a newer analogue on the scale of the global economy to old-style capitalism.

Given the globalized realities of economic life today, Kojève argues, one cannot be satisfied with looking at things simply from the standpoint of national economies or even the regional industrialized economy of Europe and America. One must see the need for "Fordizing" the global analogue of old-style capitalism, colonialism. In the long run, with a truly global economy, a political-economic structure that continues to leave the majority poor while providing further constant enrichment to a minority will not be sustainable. Accordingly, just as certain capitalists before, along with, and after Ford were able to free themselves from the short-sightedness that Marx predicted and to take effective measures to reform the capitalist political economy so as to transform it peacefully, so statesmen and economic leaders today should address the fundamental problem of global political economy, colonialism. Kojève grants that this may be the greatest political problem of the twentieth century; but in this lecture he mostly abstains from political analysis to concentrate on the economic side, and he is particularly concerned that economic actors should work to deal with this issue economically (as Ford and others did chiefly in the context of one national economy). The task of political economy globally understood, therefore, is to bring it about that all the peoples of the world share in the fruits of technological progress.

Kojève suggests that the developed world urgently needs to undertake measures to deal with this problem of colonialism, and he discusses three approaches to it. First, the developed industrialized nations could make agreements regarding terms of trade, whereby they would jointly bind themselves to paying higher prices for the products, especially raw materials, that they import from underdeveloped countries. Kojève narrates how the nations of the world negotiated, for five months in Havana in 1947–1948 and then four months more in Geneva in 1954, on an agreement to this effect, attained near unanimity, but then had to abandon it because it was rejected "for reasons of principle" by the United States (reasons which Kojève further on in the lecture admits that he could never understand and which he therefore tended to consider mere prejudice). A second approach would give direct aid to underdeveloped countries through international organizations; and here too Kojève rather satirically evokes all the talks, conferences, and meetings that have been devoted to this and the altogether tiny accomplishment that has resulted.

Finally, particular countries could direct aid to the underdeveloped countries, and here something more important has happened. Whereas most industrialized countries are colonialist, more or less consciously, in the economic sense that Kojève has defined, France according to his data now gives back (chiefly through investment) four or five times more capital to its colonies and former colonies than it takes out in surplus value. (And without claiming to have quite such precise information, he expresses his belief that England's situation is roughly comparable.) If colonialism is defined by taking from underdeveloped countries, France and England turn out to be anti-colonialist. Thus, in Kojève's summary formulation, all the industrialized countries of the world are de facto colonialist (including those who have not engaged in political colonialism, including the United States, which he considers the headquarters of such economic colonialism) except for France and England. Their example points the way to what needs to be done: colonialism needs to be transformed just as old-style capitalism was transformed. It needs to change from a *taking* colonialism to become a *giving* colonialism, one that returns the surplus value produced to the poorer areas of the world and, still better, more besides. (And one will also, Kojève notes, need to come up with a better name than "giving colonialism.") This more equal sharing, globally, of the advantages of modern technology and productivity was one of Kojève's chief practical goals in his postwar career at the French Ministry of Finance.

Near the end of his lecture Kojève reflects on the advantages of pursuing the goal of promoting development through a regional division of responsibilities. The most interesting region, especially when we think back to his 1945 proposal of a "Latin Empire" as the goal for French policy, is the European region. Harking back to this earlier proposal, he discusses the European region as the Mediterranean region, the region that once was the Roman Empire. He makes the historical point that this area was a vital and resilient economic region, which could even have continued to flourish one way or another in spite of the barbarian invasions, except that the conquests by Islam ended up turning the Mediterranean Sea from the connecting link of a single economic world into the boundary between two worlds, so that for centuries it no longer served commercial traffic but became "the showplace of warlike games." But now that men are more serious and grown up, and the time is not far off that they won't play games anymore, the promise of a reconstruction of this whole area as one economic region makes sense. Indeed, Kojève asserts that from the standpoint of a "giving colonialism," this economic region is "blessed by God." Given the demographic relationships, the developed European countries north of the Mediterranean would definitely be able to bear the burden of making the contributions necessary for the southern and eastern countries to join gainfully in the region's economic prosperity. Europe, even if considered "small" when compared to the Anglo-American sphere, has no need of assistance from afar to carry out this task at hand. Beyond the moral grounds for giving, Kojève recurs to the notion that poor customers are bad customers (thus appealing to ordinary economic self-interest) and adds an element of threat by suggesting that bad customers may even be dangerous (thus appealing to the more urgent interest in safety or self-preservation).

Since writing his proposal for a Latin Empire in 1945, Kojève had in fact seen Europe move not in his proposed direction of a Mediterranean empire but toward the European Economic Community (of France, Germany, Italy, Belgium, Netherlands, and Luxembourg). The inclusion of Germany was the really big difference from what Kojève had proposed before (when he had assumed that, in between the Slavo-Soviet and the Anglo-American empires, Germany would likely adhere to the latter); but England still stood outside the new European entity (and continued outside of it until after Kojève had passed away). Now in 1957 we see Kojève preserving an element of the older Mediterranean proposal in presenting his new views on the issue of colonialism from a broad European perspective. From today's standpoint, Kojève's tantalizingly brief mentions of the problems connected with Islamic countries in the vicinity of the Mediterranean are particularly intriguing. In his writing of 1945, Kojève had on the one hand indicated that Catholicism was an existing force for unity within the proposed Latin Empire, and that "the religious and ecclesiastical (clearly distinct from 'clerical') aspect is, in our day, anything but negligible." (104). But he went on to suggest the possibility of a Mediterranean reconciliation with Islam in this brief formulation:

> It is possible, furthermore, that it is in this unified Latino-African world that the Muslim problem (and perhaps the "colonial" problem in general) will be able to be resolved some day. For since the Crusades, Arab Islam and Latin Catholicism are united in an opposition that is synthetic from several points of view (the influence of Arabic thought on Scholasticism, the penetration of Islamic art into the Latin countries, etc.). And nothing dictates that, within a true *Empire*, this synthesis of opposites could not be freed of its internal contradictions, which are truly irreducible only so long as purely *national* interests are at stake. (107)

This lecture on political economy, twelve years later than the outline on postwar grand strategy, shows that Kojève had in the meantime continued to think about how to deal with the problem of these Islamic countries. In this chiefly economic context he points toward the possibility of their moving beyond the now pointless centuries of conflict and toward integration into a flourishing European economic region, and so becoming good customers rather than bad or even dangerous ones. Reading this discussion today, one certainly finds it easy to wish that more of the policy toward underdeveloped countries in the vicinity of the Mediterranean that Kojève sketched here had in fact been implemented.

To bring this chapter to an end, I should like to express some concluding reflections on this shift in Kojève's understanding regarding the meaning of the end of history. In a way, one can state the difference easily enough. For the earlier Kojève, the standard Marxist (or if you prefer, activist or heroic[7] Hegelian) stance applies: the end of history is somehow basically known but actually achieving it lies in the future as our project, our task, our goal, the success in achieving which is of course contingent since the human future cannot be known. For the later Kojève: Hegel was right in the first place; history ended in 1806; what happens now is the working out of details of implementation that are of less than world-historical significance. We are therefore no longer called to heroics, for instance revolutionary action with risk of life in bloody battle; philosophy (or rather, now, philosophy that has in the decisive respects become wisdom) no longer exhorts us to pursue a project of world-historical import, but rather shows us to see our true situation and have the wisdom to accept our fate. Of course, how we work out certain as yet unsettled details of the end of history has its own interest and importance. It may not be of world-historical importance, for example, that French and more broadly Latin cultural influences be preserved as something different from the American way of life, but it certainly has no small importance for how we live, for the satisfaction of or the failure to satisfy our tastes, and for the character of the activities that still constitute our work and that occupy our times of leisure.

Now, the least plausible aspect of Kojève's later view regarding the end of history is its corollary that the West and the Soviet Union are substantially the same rather than alternatives of world-historical importance. (However implausible that later view may be to ordinary common sense, it is worth remembering that Kojève was not alone in taking such a position: on the one hand, many social scientists who specialized in the communist world or in issues of development or modernization held to some kind of convergence thesis, and on the other hand Heidegger, for his own reasons, averred that there was no metaphysical difference between the Soviet Union and the United States.) But it also seems somehow implausible to say that it is not of world-historical importance whether the developed countries successfully manage through enlightened policies to lead the others peacefully toward worldwide prosperity or, failing to do so, see instead violent uprisings by the impoverished majorities against the wealthy minority. Kojève's answer to these two objections, I think, would be along these lines. Policies that are reasonably defensible all tend toward the same end state, whose foundation was laid definitively in 1806. The future is indeed contingent in many ways, but whatever the contingencies, actions of which a reasonable account can be given can all be shown to lead in fundamentally the same direction. The philosophical teaching (or if definitively true, systematic wisdom's teaching) of the end of history cannot abolish all contingency. In particular, it cannot absolutely guarantee that human beings may not choose to pursue manifestly irrational courses of action. These would produce results that in essence place us somewhere back at some earlier stage of now completed history. But, I believe Kojève would argue, this possibility does not refute his position. The inescapable fact is that neither philosophy nor wisdom can now or ever could refute the most stubborn irrationality. The most wisdom can do is to enable us to understand the whole, but not necessarily to dominate it so thoroughly as to conquer all contingency. But granting this limitation, one can nonetheless say that modern rationality does tend to provide more powerful arms on the side of reason than the unending debate between opposed positions in the premodern tradition of Western philosophy ever did.

NOTES

1. Whether it might involve espionage is considered in the epilogue.

2. *Giovanni Gentile: Mussolini's Fascist Philosopher* by M. E. Moss (New York: Peter Lang, 2004) shows a considerable number of Hegelian themes that enter into Gentile's thought.

3. This suggestion, admittedly, does point toward a permanently relevant human nature and away from the Kojèvean-Hegelian position that human being simply creates itself over historical time through the negation of nature, including the elements of nature in itself.

4. In his 1968 interview with Gilles Lapouge, he confirmed this view by elaborating that the Chinese revolution amounted only to bringing the Napoleonic Code to China.

5. Regarding the particular contempt that Kojève expressed for America and the "American way of life" (which by the way he invariably designates in English), I would say, not in defense but in mitigation, that slander or insult is most excusable when it is directed against the most powerful.

6. *The Sunday of Life*, trans. Barbara Wright (New York: New Directions Books, 1977).

7. Michael S. Roth has used this phrase to describe the Hegelianism of Jean Hyppolite in his book *Knowing and History*; I think the term can also be appropriately applied to the earlier Kojève's position regarding the end of history.

Chapter Five

Updating Hegel's System

His weekdays taken up with his work at the French Ministry of Finance, Kojève devoted weekends during the early 1950s to his philosophical writings,
which aimed at a *mise à jour*, an updating, of Hegel's system of knowledge.
From this endeavor, five volumes have been published; they constitute most of
the "Introduction" to the projected but largely unwritten updating of the
Hegelian system of knowledge or wisdom. The five volumes taken together
could be characterized as a huge elaboration of his three lectures on "Eternity,
Time, and the Concept" from the *Introduction to the Reading of Hegel* (which,
on the other hand, he restated with remarkable brevity, emphasizing above all
the role of Kant, in an article, "Le Concept et Le Temps," for an issue of *Deucalion* in 1955 devoted to Hegelianism). These volumes define and elaborate
all the fundamental notions that philosophy needs to use, such as concept,
meaning, essence, discourse, thing, general, particular, abstract, concrete, and
many more, and then proceed to categorize and to analyze the whole history
of philosophy culminating in the Hegelian transformation of Kantian philosophy into definitive knowledge. The much greater length of the five-volume
version of this argument consists chiefly in its far more detailed analyses of the
greatest past historical philosophies (of Parmenides, Plato, Aristotle, Kant, and
Hegel), as well as the detailed discussions of many others (Heraclitus,
Socrates, Democritus, Epicureans, Stoics, and Neo-Platonists, notably Ploti-
nus and Proclus).

What we have of Kojève's introduction to the *System of Knowledge* consists of five volumes. The first volume, *Le Concept, le Temps et le Discours*
(*The Concept, Time, and Discourse*), begins with an overall preface and introduction to Kojève's entire effort to update the Hegelian system, and then
proceeds to present two introductions to that system: "First Introduction to

97

the System of Knowledge: Psychological Introduction of the Concept (in accordance with Aristotle)" and "Second Introduction to the System of Knowledge: Logical Introduction of Time (in accordance with Plato)." This first volume is followed by a third historical introduction, several volumes in length. At the beginning of the first volume of this "Third Introduction," that is, in a brief "Preface" to the first of three volumes of the *Essai d'une histoire raisonnée de la philosophie païenne* (*Attempt at a Reasoned History of Pagan Philosophy*), Kojève sketches the original plan of this "Third Introduction":

> It would have been [that is to say, if it had been completed] a (reasoned) history of Philosophy as a whole, that is to say, from Thales to Hegel. This third introduction of the *System of Knowledge* would have had as its title: *Historical introduction of the concept into time as philosophical introduction of time into the concept (the situation and role of Kant in the history of Philosophy)*. (*Essai*, vol. I, 9)

After a long (150 pages) introduction to this first volume of the *Essai*, entitled "The Dialectical Structure of the History of Philosophy," which provides a rationale and a structure for dealing with the whole project of a complete history of Western philosophy, Kojève begins "Section A: The Evolution of Philosophy during the pre-Kantian Period" and soon presents a division of this Section A into three parts: "I. Antiquity and the Completion of Pagan Philosophy. II. The Middle Ages and Pagan Philosophy's Being Placed into Opposition with Judeo-Christian Theology. III. Modern Times and the Forerunners of Christian Philosophy" (*Essai*, vol. I, 195). This "Third Introduction" to the whole *System of Knowledge*, therefore, should in principle have consisted of three parts dealing with pre-Kantian philosophy, followed by a treatment of Kant. Of these three parts, we have only one that is fully completed: the three-volume *Essai d'une histoire raisonnée de la philosophie païenne*. The first volume deals with the pre-Socratics, the second with Plato and Aristotle, and the third with Hellenistic philosophy and the Neo-Platonists. The second and third parts, dealing with the philosophies of the Middle Ages and of pre-Kantian modernity, do not exist; and to complete this third introduction to the Hegelian system, we have no *Essai d'une histoire raisonnée de la philosophy chrétienne* (*Attempt at a Reasoned History of Christian Philosophy*) but only a volume on Kant, the manuscript of which was found among Kojève's papers after his death. This volume, *Kant*, now concludes this four-volume "Third Introduction" to the updating of Hegel's system.

The scope and conception of this whole multivolume project is vividly suggested by the three epigraphs (to volume I of the *Essai*) that Kojève uses. The first is from Proverbs 8.22–23: "*I (Wisdom) have been established from the beginning,* **before** *the origin of the Earth.*" The second, a fragment of Xeno-phanes, states: "*The Gods have not revealed all things to men from the be-ginning; but, through searching, they find* **with time** *what is best.*" Finally, Hegel: "*Geist* **ist** *Zeit*" ("*Spirit* **is** *Time*") (*Essai*, vol. I, 7).

From the outline alone of the five-volume, yet incomplete, introduction to the unfinished work, it is clear that this project of Kojève to develop an up-dated Hegelian System of Knowledge is the largest and most comprehensive philosophical project that he did or could envision himself engaged in carry-ing out. Perhaps for that reason, he wrote a substantial preface to it such as one does not find for his other writings (the "Preface" of *Le Concept, le Temps et le Discours*) in which, among other things, he expresses his intel-lectual debts. I have already referred, in chapter 2, to his acknowledgment of the influence of Heidegger on his capacity to understand Hegel's *Phenome-nology of Spirit*. He goes on to say:

> Having mentioned the influence of the ex-Heidegger [that is, the Heidegger of *Sein und Zeit*, before he took what Kojève held to be a bad turn] I must equally indicate that of my friends Jacob Klein and Leo Strauss (of Russian and German origin respectively, and now Americans). Without them I would not have known what Platonism is. Now, without knowing that, one does not know what philos-ophy is. (*Le Concept, le Temps et le Discours*, 33)

The affirmation that Plato is the philosopher par excellence is striking and leads one to think of two different ways of ranking philosophers. The way that one might normally think of as most typical of a progressive historicist ap-proach would tend to treat the later as superior to the earlier, on the grounds of greater closeness to the definitive truth. But another way of judging has ap-peal as perhaps more interesting and certainly more nuanced: to evaluate the power, depth, comprehensiveness, and degree of important and impressive in-novation of the philosopher's thinking (as distinguished from how near to the final truth he came). It is in this way, I think, that Kojève ranked Plato as somehow the first or the archetype of philosophers; in this he shared Niet-zsche's judgment, who characterized Plato as having "the greatest strength any philosopher so far has had at his disposal."[1] Kojève puts Kant in the high-est rank of modern philosophers (and in this respect he parts company with Nietzsche). As to whether Kant or Plato should be ranked the greater philoso-pher, Kojève considers them to be equals, as far as he can tell. Both were deeply religious, in Kojève's view, and the philosophical discoveries of both were made more effective, more available, and truer by being brought down to earth by great unreligious successors near to them in both time and space: Aristotle and Hegel. Aristotle brought the Platonic discoveries down to earth from the transcendent realm where Plato thought they existed, and Hegel analogously needed only to eliminate the Transcendent, of religious origin, from Kant's philosophy in order to transform it into definitive wisdom.[2]

No reader of these volumes can have the least doubt of their philosophical seriousness; they develop with great detail and vast learning his argument that the history of philosophy has in fact completed a circle in which all possibilities have been passed through, and they carry out this task with immensely more detailed epistemological argumentation than he presented elsewhere. And to mention right away what in my judgment may perhaps be of the greatest philosophical interest in them: these volumes seem to advance Kojève's own attempt to deal with what he saw as the greatest difficulty in Hegel's system. This difficulty, which I have discussed earlier in chapter 2 in relation to his *Introduction to the Reading of Hegel*, involves the question of how one can fill in the gap that is left when one abandons, as Kojève thought one must, Hegel's philosophy of nature. Leo Strauss raised this question in a letter to Kojève as one of his two most important objections to Kojève's position, the other being the problem of the "last man."[3] In *Introduction to the Reading of Hegel*, the closest Kojève came to proposing a solution was this:

> When specifically human error is finally transformed into the truth of absolute Science, Man ceases to exist as Man and History comes to an end. The overcoming of Man (that is, of Time, that is, of Action) in favor of static Being (that is, Space, that is, Nature), therefore, is the overcoming of Error in favor of Truth. And if History is certainly the history of human errors, Man himself is perhaps only an error of Nature that "by chance" (freedom?) was not immediately eliminated. (*Introduction to the Reading of Hegel*, 156)

It is hard to take full satisfaction in an explanation that leaves something as fundamental as the coming into being of Man (and the consequent need for a dualist ontology with a deep distinction between Nature and Man) as a consequence of chance. Now, certainly Kojève is not alone to suggest that the distinctively human arises as a consequence of chance. Jean-Jacques Rousseau suggested as much in his *Discourse on Inequality*, and chance plays an enormous role in the coming into being of things, including human beings, for thinkers going as far back as the Epicureans and Democritus. But Kojève is quite dismissive of the philosophical contribution of Epicurus, whom he characterizes as elaborating his own way of life as a model of happiness for emulation rather than developing any original contributions to philosophical discourse as such; and as we are about to see, Kojève also has serious reservation regarding the status as philosopher even of the far more original and powerful thinker, Democritus.

Kojève's systematic elaboration of the three levels needed for every genuine philosophy, and his development of the level of *energology* (the level of

objective reality, to which he had applied the term "metaphysics" in his earlier writing), seems to be a serious attempt to deal more fully with physics and
its relation to and place in a complete system of knowledge, and at least in
that respect to deal more fully with the relationship of human history to the
realm of nature. Given Kojève's rare capacity to be able to deal with both
physics and philosophy, one can only regret that his working out of this problem did not come to completion. Perhaps it may yet point the way for others.

Kojève's overall attempt to update Hegel's system is an enormous effort to
continue the philosophic tradition, in a strict and demanding sense of the term
"philosophy," which insists on three strong criteria that were first fully and adequately articulated, in his judgment, by Kant (though even Kant lacked full
clarity about the three levels or aspects, the third criterion discussed below).
First, Kojève insists that philosophy must be discursive knowledge; other
nondiscursive representations of reality, such as the mathematical representations of modern physics, are not truly philosophy, according to Kojève.
Physics using mathematics represents objective reality through equations,
which he often calls algorithms as distinguished from discursive accounts. If
one tries to state modern physics' view of objective reality in philosophical
discourse, one ends up saying incoherent or contradictory things. One must
say, for instance, that the same thing is both a particle localized in space and
a wave extending infinitely throughout all of space. This works satisfactorily
within the context of the elaboration and application of physics as a mathematical representation or algorithm, but falls short of being coherent discourse.

Second, Kojève also insists, and no less firmly, on that Kantian element of
a definition of philosophy that insists that philosophy is a self-reflexive form
of knowledge, knowledge that can give an account of itself. Philosophy is a
form of knowledge that not only gives a coherent discursive account of some
area of being, but also addresses the question of *how* it can give such an account and how *it* can give such an account; the philosopher speaks of what he
knows along with how he can know it, and what he himself is so as to be engaged in such knowing.

Third, Kojève's analysis also insists on another aspect of authentic philosophy: to be complete and systematic, philosophy must develop an argument
always on three levels. In his Hegel seminar, Kojève had called those three
levels phenomenology (the level of our experience of the spatial-temporal
world, empirical-Existence), metaphysics (the objective-Reality of things),
and ontology (the fundamental structure of being that underlies the objective
world, or given-Being). In this work of the 1950s, Kojève keeps the terms
"phenomenology" and "ontology" but uses a new term, "energology,"[4] to des-
ignate the intermediate level. He does not discuss how he invented this term,

but it seems reasonable to understand it from its Greek roots. They reflect the Aristotelian distinction between *dunamis* (potentiality) and *energeia* (being at work [*ergon*], actuality or actualization or reality or realization). On the level of energology (objective reality), things are real or actual, not potential, possible, or the like.

To elaborate these three aspects of being, and therefore three levels of philosophical discourse, is a difficult matter, which Kojève pursues in his analyses of all the philosophers that he discusses (often to show how they blurred the distinctions, or drew them not quite accurately—even in the case of Kant). A brief general statement that he makes in the *Kant* volume helps to show what he means by these three levels:

> It is by "reducing" (through "abstraction") Extension-Duration to Space-Time that we "reduce" empirical-Existence (which alone is given or revealed in an *immediate* fashion in and by Perception taken as a whole) to objective-Reality (given in and by the Sensation of the variation of the Tonus of that Perception), and it is in "reducing" Space-Time (or, more exactly, Extension-Duration) to Spatio-Temporality that we "reduce" objective-Reality (or, more exactly, empirical-Existence) to given-Being (revealed in and by the Sentiment of Well- or Ill-Being that is implicated in Perception). (*Kant*, 202)

In other words: the totality of what is, is the whole spatially extended and temporally enduring world of our empirical existence that is revealed to us through Perception and discursively articulated by phenomenology. The other levels, objective-Reality and given-Being, are arrived at by abstraction; they are different aspects of the same world (philosophical knowledge does not grasp anything eternal or transcendent, in the sense of outside this spatial-temporal world). The level of objective-Reality (dealt with by "energology") is given to us not by the "*content* of Perception or 'Sensation'" (which reveals empirical-Existence to us) but by "the *fact* of the *variation* of the 'Tonus' of Perception or of 'Sensation'" (*Kant*, 159). Since Kojève also accepts the definition of Maine de Biran and others that the real is what resists (*Introduction to the Reading of Hegel*, 156), I think we can understand "the variation of Tonus of Perception" to mean the variation in the intensity of any (or all) of the sense perceptions (for instance, not only that you touch something and you feel its solidity, but that when you push harder, you feel it resist your push harder). This aspect of objective-Reality, which physics measures, is constituted by the notion of irreducible opposition: of real to unreal, positive to negative (in electrical charge), the full ("Matter") and the empty ("Rayonnement," radiation) (*Kant*, 159n1). The third level, the aspect of given-Being (dealt with by ontology), is given or revealed to us "in and by the Sentiment of Well- or Ill-Being that is implicated in Perception." Thus our total experience of things includes the content of Perceptions, the awareness of the variation in the Tonus of Perceptions, and the Sentiment of Well- or Ill-Being involved in the Perceptions. What seems surprising at first blush, I think, is that this last Sentiment seems perhaps too subjective, too variable from one person to another, and not on its face "philosophical" enough to reveal to us the fundamental or ontological level of given-Being. But in fact it makes sense in this way: Hegelian Ontology involves the elaboration of the aspects of Being as Identity, Negativity, and Totality; and it is Negativity that is distinctive of the free historical human individual. Now, the experience of Negativity is one of Ill-Being: a sense that something is unsatisfactory (wrong, defective, or whatever) in our experience of Being; and in the context of that experience, we may then respond with a free human reaction to it: religious thinking, for example, or revolutionary action.[5] This Sentiment of Well- or Ill-Being, then, characterizes most fundamentally the mode of our being-in-the-World, is at the source of our Negativity and historical action, and in that sense is the way that the aspect of given-Being is "given or revealed" to us; this formulation also, not surprisingly, seems to reintroduce on a Hegelian nontranscendent basis the old Platonic notion of the primacy of the Good.

Kojève is well aware that not all thinkers generally recognized as philosophers have known and accepted the definition that he insists on; for the great philosophers, however, he tries to show that they did in fact develop their arguments on all three levels even if they were not altogether conscious of doing so and even if this three-level structure was not an explicit theme for them. He also recognizes, however, that their lack of full self-consciousness about the threefold distinction of levels of philosophical discourse (and aspects of being) leads them sometimes to develop their arguments with less clarity than they might have been able to attain. His definition of philosophy is so demanding, however, that he characterizes certain thinkers generally called philosophers in the tradition as something else.

Most notable in this respect, I think, and most interesting for its bearing on the relation of philosophy and physics, is his treatment of Democritus. For Kojève, Democritus is not really a philosopher, above all because he does not develop arguments on all three levels. He takes the level of objective reality (and explanation relating to that level, energology) to be the whole of being that needs to be accounted for in addition to the experienced phenomena themselves. He is indeed a great thinker, but not a philosopher; in Kojève's judgment he was the first clear elaborator of physical science, who gives explanations on the level of energology (which he generally confused with ontology). He is, according to Kojève, the first thinker to give a clear account of what objective reality is, as distinguished from the phenomena as we experience them empirically. He fell short of being a philosopher in that he took objective reality to be given-Being; and in consequence, he could not give anything like an even apparently satisfactory account of how it is that we can give a discursive account of all things, including our knowledge of ourselves as philosophic knowers (in addition to our knowing the objective reality of things). But the aspect of being that Kojève calls objective reality had escaped the other pre-Socratic philosophers. In elaborating it, and developing an account of the nature of objective realities (atoms, space, motion), Democritus laid the foundations of a structure that came to fulfillment only with modern physics, of which he is therefore the distant progenitor. For Democritus, things happen on the level of, or in their aspect of, objective reality through necessity and through chance; in fact chance and necessity in his thought are really two terms for or perspectives on the same thing (as Aristotle points out), and they are the analogue to modern quantum physics' law of statistical determination (*Essai*, vol. I, 320). A final quote will put into evidence the high regard in which Kojève holds Democritus as physicist:

> But if he [Aristotle] speaks of objective-Reality as a philosopher, that is to say by inserting it in between Being and Existence, whereas Democritus speaks of it as a Physicist, that is to say as the unique infrastructure of this latter [viz. Existence], Democritus nevertheless speaks of objective-Reality far more correctly (and more "scientifically") than Aristotle. This case shows to what extent Philosophy had trouble in *speaking* of the Reality that Physics *measures*. It is only in our day that it has become possible to speak of it in a truly satisfactory fashion. (*Essai*, vol. I, 356)

In discussing Democritus, Kojève presents a general reflection on thinkers who make important contributions to philosophy without being philosophers themselves; the most important are religious types or theologians, on the one hand, and physicists (in the broad sense of inquirers into the objective realities of nature), on the other. Kojève's own intellectual development seems to have reflected this insight in advance, as it were; for as we saw in chapter 1, the topics of religion, of atheism or theism, and of physics were what absorbed his interest, in addition to philosophy itself, earlier in his life. Now in the 1950s he writes:

> Regarding *Theologians*, their philosophical role (somehow unconscious and involuntary) consisted essentially in drawing Philosophy's attention from time to time to the presence in the Universe of the *sui generis* phenomenon that is the "individual" and "free," or rather "historical" *human existence*, which the philosophers left to themselves "ignore" too easily, even if they do not go so far as purely and simply to deny it. As for the *Physicists*, they play the same role as regards the equally *sui generis* "aspect" of the Universe (or rather of the Cosmos-of-which-one-speaks in the World-in-which-one-speaks) that is *objective-Reality*, as op-

posed both to given-Being and "phenomenal" empirical-Existence. (*Essai*, vol. I, 300)

In the history of philosophy, according to Kojève, the meaning of the notion "objective-Reality" is rather poorly defined before Kant, but Democritus first discovered this aspect of the Universe and showed it completely to the Philosophers.

From such genuinely and fully discursive knowledge, which as philosophic is able to give a full account of its own possibility and develops its account of things on all three levels, Kojève distinguishes science, both physical and social. He maintains the position he took in his *Introduction to the Reading of Hegel*, that modern physical science is not truly discursive; its mathematical expressions are algorithmic rather than discursive (and hence modern physics is energometry; energology would include the discursive account of how such physics is possible for a concrete human being, and is not part of modern physics itself but a necessary part of philosophy). Physics is a specialized science devoted to rational knowledge of its object, the physical objective reality of things. Were a physicist to try to give a full discursive account of how he can know what he studies, and what he himself is in order to be able to pursue such knowledge, he would necessarily have to move from the pursuit of physics to philosophy (with, therefore, no guarantee of success, however successful he may be as a physicist). A philosopher needs to understand the level of objective-Reality and hence physics but should certainly not expect sound guidance in philosophy proper from physicists as such: "Every Philosopher must take account and give an account of the *Physics* of his time, even if he rejects the supposedly 'philosophical' ideas of *Physicists* in general and of contemporary Physicists in particular" (*Kant*, 187).

Insofar as the social sciences try to model themselves on modern natural science, according to Kojève's account, they apply (at their most rigorous) energometry or phenomenometry to human affairs, and energography or phenomenography when they fall short of real measurement. These sciences are not for that reason false or lacking value, but they are not discursive knowledge that could satisfy a philosophic desire to know. When they turn from imitating the methods and mathematical expressions of natural science to formulating their research and findings in discursive speech, they exhibit, or fall under, the anti-philosophic principle that the concept is temporal; they are distant descendants of Heraclitus, the Sophists, skeptics, and relativists of all sort. Whether of the sociological, historical, or psychological variant, they necessarily participate in the "endless chattering" that alone is possible on a basis that rejects the possibility of philosophical truth (*Essai*, vol. I, 34–57).

Kojève's clear distinction between philosophical knowing and sociological or psychological explanation is touched on and put to an amusing use at the end of his "Preface" to *Le Concept, le Temps et le Discours*. He notes that one could easily establish that, from the standpoint of the science of sociology, his book is equivalent to an attempt to "justify" discursively the events that began to develop in Moscow in 1917 and "which have exerted a definite (*certain*) attraction on certain (*certains*) of my Russian or other contemporaries, myself included." Similarly, from the standpoint of the science of psychology, it is not hard to see that someone who takes note of the fact, toward the end of a life devoted in major part to discourse, that he has not been able to say anything that is *inédit* (unpublished, previously unheard, new), "is naturally inclined to say what I say in my book, namely that all the discursive possibilities have been exhausted even before he has begun to speak himself." But neither of these explanations constitutes any kind of philosophical critique: they explain to some extent why it was Kojève in particular who may have said what he said; they do not provide criteria for judging the truth or success of his discourse, which could only be furnished by philosophical argumentation (*Le Concept, le Temps et le Discours*, 35–36).

The four volumes of the history of philosophy, three pagan and one Christian (the volume on Kant), are history of a special Hegelian type. Kojève does of course discuss, with impressive learning, the texts of these philosophers. But there is also a sense in which he is not as fully interested in what each of them thought, understood as exactly, comprehensively, and precisely as possible, as a historian of philosophy might be. He does not, for instance, aspire to Leo Strauss's goal of understanding each thinker as he understood himself.[6] This fact is most in evidence in his way of talking about the greatest of those philosophers, Plato. Plato's dialogues obviously yield up their meaning with considerable difficulty; the proof is that, as all serious scholars of Plato know, interpretations of the meaning of his dialogues differ greatly. In fact, we have reason to believe (and Kojève says as much in his discussion of Plato in the second volume of the *Essai*) that such differences were already being discussed during the lifetime of Plato himself and that he chose not to intervene authoritatively to resolve them. But if, as I earlier quoted Kojève as seeming to say in the "Preface" to *Le Concept, le Temps et le Discours*, Plato is perhaps the greatest of all philosophers, why would Kojève not want to be sure to have understood his thought as precisely as possible in the way in which he himself meant it?

The answer depends on two other considerations that loom larger in Kojève's thinking than this goal of historical exactitude or scrupulous adherence to the author's own intention and meaning. First, his historical approach makes him most interested in the actual effect of the philosopher's thinking on the historical development of philosophy. For that reason, for example, he states explicitly that what Aristotle said Plato meant might be more important than what Plato actually said or what the genuine meaning is for Plato of something he wrote, if the Aristotelian view of Plato's meaning prevailed in what was chiefly transmitted to posterity. (This would especially be the case, it seems to me, if—as I believe to be the case—in certain respects Plato was more skeptical, more allusive, or more complex than later traditions of Platonism, Aristotelian or other, took him to have been.) Now, Kojève does in fact often display eagerness to figure out exactly what Plato meant in a given dialogue; but in the context of introducing the Hegelian *System of Knowledge*, from the standpoint of which Kojève believes he knows that Plato's philosophy has been surpassed, the other more historicist approach takes precedence.

Secondly, Kojève develops his historical account with a schematic view in mind of how it must have developed (the earlier version of which was "Eternity, Time and the Concept" in *Introduction to the Reading of Hegel*). This is of course unavoidable for a Hegelian, who by definition views Hegel's philosophy as superior to all the alternatives, precisely because it provides, or rather is, a rationally structured integration of all past philosophy (as a crucial, indeed the most important, aspect of the rationally structured, integrated account of all past history). And so one could say that when Kojève undertakes his own history of philosophy, he already has in mind a whole structure of the dialectical development of the history of philosophy that furnishes him with a number of ideal types of philosophical positions, and that he then proceeds to seek to match up actual historical philosophers with these types. Sometimes, in fact, he indicates that the actual philosopher may not have developed as fully or as clearly as possible the position that Kojève has assigned to him. In other words, sometimes Kojève is quite explicit about his own claim to understand a philosopher substantially better than the philosopher can have understood himself. And in a way, of course, this would necessarily be true and should most certainly be welcomed if in fact Hegel's system, as a coherent account of the whole historical development of philosophy, is indeed true. No earlier philosopher could have had quite so clear and adequate an understanding of what he was doing as Hegel (and Kojève) can attain later.

Now of course this whole enterprise depends on the possibility that Hegel/Kojève can have surveyed the whole historical development of philosophy in such a way as to see that it has come to a completion through a process that has caused it to pass through all the real philosophical possibilities. This can be put in evidence by rationally deducing all the philosophical positions and showing that they correspond to the actual historical development of philosophy. (Kojève takes pains to point out that this "deduction" is anything but deduction *a priori*; it is deduction—or really more a kind of rational reconstruction—*a posteriori*, after the fact, possible therefore only when the process has actually been completed.) Now, Hegel's systematic account in fact deals only with Western philosophy, from the Greeks on down to himself. But is there not the possibility that some other philosophical position, developed elsewhere than in the West, for instance in Asia, presents an alternative that does not fit into the Hegelian schema?

Kojève deals with this problem near the beginning of this whole intellectual project (*Essai*, vol. I, 163–164). He refers to the philosophies to be found in Japan, China, and India as by general agreement most likely to be of such importance. Certainly Kojève is far better equipped than most people, including Hegel, to deal with this question of the possible challenge that Asian philosophy might pose to the Hegelian philosophic system. Most scholars of Asian language and culture are relatively ignorant of philosophy, and most (Western) philosophers (including Hegel) knew little of the Orient and especially its languages. By contrast, Kojève's early interest in Buddhism and other Asian religious philosophies led him to study the languages and literature with a philosophical intent. He cannot, of course, prove the historical negative that no such philosophy overlooked by Hegel exists, but he reports some plausible grounds for thinking that nothing crucial to the Hegelian system has been missed. His findings, briefly reported, are that Japanese philosophy offers nothing much of interest not to be found in Chinese philosophy. Regarding Chinese philosophy, he is not sure that it really deserves the name philosophy, except for the case of Buddhism, which is of Indian origin. Having studied Indian philosophy in considerable depth, he assures his readers that he has found nothing that is not also to be found, in essence, in one or another Greek philosopher.

This, however, does not mean that studying Indian philosophy, notably the Buddhist philosophy, is unrewarding; quite to the contrary, and Kojève presents a lively account of what he found valuable for himself from such study. The Hindu "genius" involves powerful imagination and "near total absence of *bon sens*" (good sense or prudence), so that:

> The philosophers of India have sometimes developed certain "western" philosophical themes with a "rigor," or rather with a "radicalism," that one has never been able or willing to attain in the West. Accordingly the Indian replicas are sometimes more "revealing" than the western originals. . . .
>
> In particular, it is thanks to this Hindu "radicalism" that one was able to constitute in India the phenomenon that is virtually unique in the world of a genuine radically *atheistic religion*, universally known under the name of Buddhism. . . . The study of Buddhist writings (which I engaged in during long years) is extremely fruitful both for the ("philosophical" or other) understanding of Religion and of Theology, and for the elucidation of certain properly philosophical, or rather Hegelian, problems. (*Essai*, vol. I, 164)

Kojève thus acknowledges valuable influence on his own thinking from the study of Indian philosophy, especially Buddhism, while explaining why he has not found it necessary to develop detailed analyses of Oriental philosophies or comparisons of them with Western philosophies in his present project. An especially interesting example of what he gained from his study of Buddhism comes up in his discussion of Kant (*Kant*, 46–50). Kojève develops an argument that the foundation of Kant's moral teaching is ultimately religious, resting on Kant's profound religious conviction (given expression in his moral philosophy) that genuine satisfaction in this world is impossible. Buddhism has a similar conviction, but as atheistic it looks not to reward by God (as union or reunion with God in a world beyond this temporal-spatial one after death), but to annihilation, the Nothingness, as the ultimate good to be attained. Kojève reflects on how, in a Buddhist culture, Kant might have developed his philosophy more fully in an atheistic manner; but in the Christian theistic context of Kant's actual world, his religiousness led to certain theological assertions, even though in the mode of an as-if, which stand in tension with the main lines of his philosophy. The final resolution of these tensions, of course, would be effected by Hegel.

The overall schema of the history of philosophy that Kojève presents starts with the question of the possibility of philosophy, posed by "Thales"; this can be called the hypothesis of philosophy. The first answer, the thesis, is due to Parmenides, with his identification of the Concept with Being in the fullest sense, Eternity. Against that thesis stands the antithesis, attributed to "Heraclitus," that philosophy is impossible because the Concept is temporal and the beings of the world all in flux.[7] Given the deep problem of these two contradictory positions, subsequent philosophy is parathetical: that is, it tries to support some part of the thesis and some part of the antithesis. Plato is parathetical with predominance of the thesis; Aristotle with predominance of the antithesis. Parathetical philosophical positions can fall anywhere along a line of more or less thetical (or antithetical) predominance. Eventually Kant develops a synthetical parathesis, which through Hegel's last step is transformed into the definitive synthesis.

In correspondence to this structure of philosophical positions, Kojève sketches the following historical periods of philosophy. After the great four ancients, Parmenides-Heraclitus and Plato-Aristotle, ancient philosophers continued to develop more or less thetical or antithetical paratheses (such as the Stoics, who combined elements of both Plato and Aristotle, though more the latter). Then Christian theology, dealing with the Incarnation, came into the world; it was not at its origin philosophical. Medieval philosophers restated the various types of ancient philosophy in the context of a world informed by

Christian theology: the patristic philosophers restated Neo-Platonic eclecti-
cism, the first scholastics went back to Plato, and of course the second scholastics like St. Thomas restated Aristotle. Then in the modern period, starting, let's
say, with Descartes, we find the first authentic philosophers to introduce Christian theological dogma (the Incarnation) into (pagan) philosophical discourse,
or rather, "to transform Christian theological Discourse into (Christian) philosophic Discourse." This endeavor was completed by Kant, who thus "synthe-
sized the (pagan) thetical and antithetical Paratheses, not 'immediately,' but
through the 'mediation' that was their 'Christianization' by pre-Kantian 'modern' philosophers" (*Essai*, vol. I, 184–185 [n32 to 154]).

It may seem strange to the reader that I have devoted only a rather short
chapter of the present book to discuss this most extensive written work of Kojève. The explanation, of course, is that my central focus in this book is on his
political thought. The project of updating Hegel's system, under discussion
here, was Kojève's most fully developed treatment of the most fundamental
issues of philosophy taken in the most general and comprehensive sense. This
project does of course have a political bearing, in that assurance, rather than
doubt, about the adequacy of a Hegelian philosophical account of all things
would most definitely have the most important political (as well as moral)
consequences; but the political dimensions of Hegelianism are treated by Kojève in more detail in the other works that I have discussed at proportionately
greater length. In regard to this complex and massive philosophical project,
accordingly, I have not attempted to say something about each major section
of each volume, but have for the most part picked out very selectively for
brief discussion arguments presented in these five volumes that contribute to
understanding the issues that arose in earlier chapters, such as the relation of
philosophy to theology and to physics.

Having said this, I certainly wish nonetheless in conclusion to express my
own judgment that this introduction to the Hegelian *System of Knowledge* is
indeed a most impressive philosophical writing, magisterial, vast in its learning, and daring in its attempt toward comprehensiveness. At one point Kojève
discusses the way to interpret philosophers; he expresses regret over scholars'
excessive concentration on the phases of development of a philosopher's
thought. This emphasis, indeed, has become virtually an obsession especially
with interpreters of Plato, who are forever trying to speculate on how his
thought changed from one dialogue to another; one could sometimes even
imagine, from the Platonic scholarship of our times, that Plato's thought en-
tered a new phase with each dialogue. Kojève admits, of course, that many
philosophers' thoughts do indeed exhibit some more or less fundamental
changes, some important differences in different periods of their activity. But
until relatively recently, philosophers tended to publish only completed and

perfected works; if the philosopher had written just a sketch or a *brouillon* (a rough draft), he would hold it back, work on it further, perfect it, before publishing it. A different approach to publishing, Kojève writes, came into being with Schelling, and it is his example and influence that has led historically oriented scholars to concentrate so much on endeavoring to display the evolution of whatever philosopher they are studying. It was Schelling who first found it choiceworthy to share writings at every stage of his thinking with the reading public, to let us into the process of the development of his thinking, to publish rough drafts. It was said of him that he underwent his apprenticeship in public. At the end of this discussion Kojève adds, in square brackets, that his own present book is such a *brouillon* (*Essai*, vol. I, 183n29). Thus he confirms, modestly, what he had said in the "Preface" to *Le Concept, le Temps et le Discours*:

> For various reasons, certain of which are perhaps valid, this book was written hastily, although I had worked on it for ten years. If I had devoted more time to its drafting, I would probably have been able to improve its form. As it is, the book is very badly drafted and it contains numerous imperfections, not only in form but also as to the substance. It would be superfluous to enumerate them: the reader will not fail to notice them himself and I ask him to excuse me for them. (*Le Concept, le Temps et le Discours*, 29)

Kojève does seem quite sincerely to regret the not fully perfected character of this writing, which he acknowledges with becoming (and rare) modesty. He had, moreover, spoken or written similarly on several occasions about his regret that *Introduction à la Lecture de Hegel* was far less perfected in form than it might have been. At the same time, he ironically attributes to his reader the capacity to articulate whatever shortcomings not only of form but even of substance might be in the book. I would have to say, for my part at least, that this is not always so easy to do. However that may be, the books display a combination of vast philosophical ambition with incomplete execution. Of the *Exposé du Systeme du Savoir* (*Exposition of the System of Knowledge*) that these volumes are meant to introduce, Bernard Hesbois has established the bare outline or table of contents. Kojève had envisioned three sections:

> The *First Section* should have articulated the fundamental concepts of *Ontology*, of *Energology*, and of *general* or *abstract Phenomenology*. The *Second Section* should have been a *specific* or *applied* and *concrete Phenomenology*, which would have presented the particular concepts of *Cosmology*, of *Biology* and of *Anthropology*. The *Third Section*, entitled *Analysis of Discourse*, should have closed the loop by making explicit the *practical*, *theoretical* and *philosophical* modalities of human discourse. An *Appendix* should have completed the Exposition by presenting a theory of *Silence* as the limit of Discourse. Finally, the

book should have come to completion with an *Afterword* that was supposed to convince the reader to have the *wisdom* to take the *End of History* "philosophically."

Beyond the introductions that we have been discussing, what have in fact been found among Kojève's papers are "an outline of the Ontology and fragments of the Energology, of the Analysis of Discourse and of the Afterword."[8]

NOTES

1. Friedrich Nietzsche, *Beyond Good and Evil*, trans. Walter Kaufman (New York: Random House, 1966), part five, section 191.

2. *Le Concept, le Temps et le Discours*, 81–83. In *Kant* (50) Kojève describes Hegel as being, like Aristotle, "profoundly unreligious." He notes that as Buddhism proves the possibility of atheistic religion, the young, still Platonizing, and hence theistic Aristotle was unreligious, thus proving the possibility of unreligious theism.

3. Letter of September 11, 1957. *On Tyranny*, 291.

4. In his discussion of Democritus, he refers without elaboration to his own proposal to "rebaptize" the rational account of the intermediate level of objective reality, between given-Being and the empirical existence of the phenomena, as "energology" (*Essai*, vol. I, 304).

5. Kojève suggests that the religious man experiences the world as irretrievably unsatisfactory, and considers Kant to exemplify this way of being in the world. By contrast, the artist (including the poet) is the opposite of the religious man: even suffering in the world can be the subject of a beautiful painting (*Kant*, 44n).

6. That Kojève was nonetheless sympathetic to this goal finds expression in an article he wrote in the 1950s for a *festschrift* in honor of Strauss (first published in English translation in *Ancients and Moderns: Essays on the Tradition of Political Philosophy in Honor of Leo Strauss*, ed. Joseph Cropsey [New York: Basic Books, 1964]). It is particularly interesting to note that Kojève accepts with no apparent reluctance Strauss's teaching on the esotericism of many philosophic authors. This acceptance is especially noteworthy if my impression is correct that scholars who take a historical approach to the study of philosophy have often been passionately hostile to the possible validity of Strauss's position on this matter. That hostility, I think, arises from the fact that such scholars characteristically wish to maintain the position that every thinker is somehow the child of his time and consequently subject to limitations on his possible understanding of things (from which the later scholar, happily, is free). Strauss's position, by contrast, suggests that the philosophic writer may well defer on the surface to the dominant opinions of his society while conveying his real philosophic thought, which is critical of those opinions, only between the lines; Strauss suggests, in consequence, that some readings of philosophers as children of their times may well be superficial readings. Now Kojève too maintains, in a Hegelian philosophic manner and contrary to the ancient stance, that thinkers do indeed sustain

a definite and crucially important relationship to the spirit of their times; but he is nonetheless open to the philosophic thinker's capacity to achieve authentic intellectual freedom. (A few people have commented that Kojève's occasionally ironical tone in this article suggests that he is satirizing Strauss's argument, but I do not believe this to be the case. Rather, it seems to me that Kojève's irony in regard to the philosophers' stance of protecting the salutary ignorance of the many through a partial camouflage of their philosophic teachings does not mock Strauss's position but rather gently ridicules the philosophers who took their own wisdom to be more exalted and certain than it truly was.)

7. Kojève explains why he puts the names "Thales" and "Heraclitus" in quotation marks. Of Thales too little is known to be certain that he really posed the philosophical question. But since someone must have done, since Parmenides was seeking to develop a philosophic response, why not go along with the tradition and call the person "Thales"? As for Heraclitus, Kojève admits that his writings are so fragmentary and obscure that they could be interpreted pretty much any way one would like; however, he thinks that the indications in Plato and Aristotle support putting Heraclitus into the philosophical position to which Kojève (and much of the tradition) assigned him (*Essai*, vol. I, 140–142).

8. Bernard Hesbois, "Présentation," *Le Concept, le Temps et le Discours*, 24–25.

Chapter Six

Conclusions

To conclude this account of Alexandre Kojève's political thought, it is natural to try to restate its basic character and to evaluate its lasting importance. I have sought to clarify the basic character of his thought throughout the previous chapters, but I have saved one major issue to address in conclusion: namely, what is the significance of Kojève's changed position regarding the end of history? Does his thought remain a rational Hegelianism, or does the later Kojève become a postmodern ironist?

As for the lasting importance of his thought, it is in this context that I shall discuss further his debate with Leo Strauss, published in the volume *On Tyranny*. I have discussed most of Kojève's writings roughly in the chronological order in which he wrote them; but I have saved some important issues in his exchange with Leo Strauss for this concluding chapter, for two reasons. First, since Kojève wrote "L'Action politique des philosophes" ("The Political Action of Philosophers") at just about the time when he was changing from being an activist or militant Hegelian to his later stance as a Hegelian who viewed history as in fact completed, one might reasonably expect his writing at this moment to state what is somehow most important and unchanging in his views. Secondly, Kojève's critique of Strauss's attempt to revive the classical philosophic approach provides a context wherein one can see most clearly the sense in which Kojève's position is a fundamental alternative in the history of philosophy; furthermore, his debate with Strauss brings most clearly into view those features of his Hegelian thinking that stand out as most important in contrast to the classical philosophy that he is rejecting.

Turning to the question of whether his Hegelian rationalism continues unabated or is replaced by postmodern irony, I can easily appreciate why people might tend to think of Kojève as a postmodern ironist, and indeed I have considerable sympathy with that point of view.[1] No one, certainly, could fail to see the playful and ironical tone of many of his statements, especially comments about the end of history that he made in his later period, such as in his articles on the novels of Raymond Queneau and of Françoise Sagan, or in remarks that several of his friends reported in which he suggested that, given the fact of the end of history, he (and his comprehending interlocutors) were no longer human beings but gods (albeit mortal gods). (And reportedly he would assign different Greek god identities to different interlocutors: Apollo to Maurice Merleau-Ponty, etc.) But playfulness is by no means limited to postmodernists; one need only remind oneself of the assertion by Plato's Athenian Stranger in *The Laws* that what is most serious about us is our playfulness or that we are playthings of the gods. In "The Emperor Julian and His Art of Writing," Kojève himself recognizes and discusses the playfulness of many philosophers. And of course irony need not be postmodern either. Surely Kojève is ironical, but so was the Platonic Socrates. In the last letter we have that was written by Kojève to Leo Strauss (*On Tyranny*, 307–308), he describes a public lecture in which his listeners treated him like a respectable professorial authority whose utterances they should take down as dogma despite his efforts to say outrageous things to provoke them. But once again, outrageous provocation is not specifically postmodern: here too it suffices to think of Socrates' provocations of Thrasymachus and Callicles in the *Republic* and the *Gorgias* respectively.

Setting aside for the moment implications that might be drawn from his practical activities (which are always open to conflicting possible interpretations), one must note, most importantly, that against the notion of Kojève's no longer being truly serious about his Hegelian system stands the manifest seriousness of his writings from the fifties that sought to constitute an introduction to his updating of the Hegelian system, which have been the subject of discussion in the preceding chapter. Above all, unlike postmodernists, Kojève seems ever to remain the staunch enemy of relativism (and in this respect, of course, he shared a fundamental agreement with Leo Strauss, toward whom otherwise he stood as a fundamental philosophical antagonist). The five-volume introduction makes it perfectly clear that the later Kojève is no less fundamentally concerned with making sense of how we can have Truth in the strong sense of the term than the earlier Kojève of *Introduction to the Reading of Hegel*. The notion that the Concept could be understood as temporal (as Heraclitus held, followed in this by his sophistic offspring and by relativistic skeptics of all kinds ever since) is exactly what the philosophic tradition ever tries to rise above, in Kojève's account. Kojève's rejection of this notion of a temporal concept, by which genuinely philosophical inquiry into the problem of Truth is necessarily abandoned, is nowhere stated more clearly than in a long sentence relating to Kant from his 1955 article "Le Concept et Le Temps," which I have quoted once already but consider worth quoting again:

> The *temporal* so-called "concept," i.e. a concept by definition *variable* and thus multiple and varied, is in effect nothing but the aggregation of the "notions" with which men have peopled the world since they began to speak in it and which allow them to fabricate the discourses that non-philosophers of all types make everywhere and since always in order to communicate mutually with each other, with a view to making them "recognize" the different "personal opinions" that they *have*, to be sure, and to which they *hold* with more or less *conviction*, *faith* or *force*, but of which it is absolutely impossible to say whether they are *true* or *false*, although one can draw conclusions about their "orthodoxy" or "heterodoxy" by establishing their "success" or their "failure" in the natural and historical *given* world in which they are emitted. (14)

In chapter 4 I discussed some features of the later Kojève's often ironically stated view of life at the end of history. But do these ironical statements amount to a turn from rationalism to postmodern irony?[2] I would argue the negative. The end of history is for Kojève both rationally comprehensible as the outcome of the completed historical process and rationally understandable as a state, the only state known to us, in which one has good and sufficient reason to be satisfied. It is to the credit, I think, of Kojève's intellectual honesty and intransigence that he clarifies certain problematic consequences of that end state. It is true, for example, that certain aspects of the past that one might find admirable may no longer make sense at the end of history—all those relating to warlike valor, for instance. But can anyone reasonably wish to re-create the past circumstances where those traits were most highly prized? Surely one can make the case that it is preferable to live now, at a time when, to understand the world, one needs to know its whole past history, including the different human excellences that may have prevailed in other epochs, while not necessarily having to practice them in the present. Can one reasonably want to re-create the circumstances of a past, whose shortcomings and contradictions led men to reject it and move on to a later historical epoch? Anyone can of course imagine this or that feature of a past epoch that he would like to see existing in the present; but it would be quite a different matter to be able to go beyond entertaining that kind of whim and actually to make a rational argument that the past epoch is to be preferred to the present.

But what about the possibility that posthistorical men would degenerate into the "last men" deplored by Nietzsche? (This, after all, was the question that Strauss raised in objection to Kojève's position, along with the problem of what could replace Hegel's rejected philosophy of nature.[3]) When Kojève

writes of the possible descent of human beings into animality, is he not con-
ceding the merit of Nietzsche's argument about the last man? Surely a hard
question, and once again, it is one that Kojève himself raises. But let us remember that he does not assert that mankind has descended into animality. He
does once, it is true, literally claim to see that that outcome is "a present reality" in the United States, but however deep a distaste for the "American way
of life" the comment may display, it is clearly something—like many casual
remarks by Kojève about particular persons, countries, events, and so on—
that needs to be taken *cum salis grano*, with a grain of salt, and not with grim
literalness (as he said explicitly at one point in his Düsseldorf lecture, shortly
after referring to Washington as the headquarters of "colonialism on principle"). And his brief ironical sketches of what may be missing at the end of
history, as I argued in chapter 4, cannot really be taken as foreclosing the possible continuation of our humanity, although they most certainly do force us
to rethink for ourselves what the preservation of our humanity might require
of us.[4] And finally, to refer briefly to what I bracketed earlier—it seems to me
that Kojève's remarkable energy and concentration on his philosophical and
practical tasks cannot easily be thought to comport with a stance of postmodern irony. His central concern with bringing underdeveloped countries into
the world system of economic prosperity surely bespeaks a rational modernist
rather than a postmodernist orientation, for one would expect a postmodernist
to be rather more entranced by the charms of the other, more drawn to value
difference, and less enthusiastic about bringing the fruits of Western modernity to third world or underdeveloped or backward areas.

While thus disinclined to view Kojève as a postmodern ironist, I do tend to
find an ultimate irony in the development of his thought, in the following
sense. In the final analysis, I suspect, he may be more a philosopher (like
Plato) than a wise man (as Hegel appears to have believed he became), while
keeping up the pose of a Hegelian wise man because of his genuine philosophic judgment that Hegel's position is more persuasive, explains the human
phenomena more fully, and provides a fuller and more coherent account of
the possibility of philosophy than Plato's. In the last letter that Kojève wrote
to Leo Strauss that has been found and published, he told about his having
given a lecture on dialectics to an overflow crowd at the Collège
Philosophique of Jean Wahl; Kojève expressed his disappointment with the
reaction of passive acceptance on the part of his audience, and then wrote as
follows: "All this in order to tell you that I am becoming more and more 'platonic.' One should address the few, not the many. One should speak and write
as little as possible. Unfortunately my *Attempt at a Reasoned History of Pagan Philosophy* is to be published, and it comprises more than 1000 (sic)
pages!"[5] This is a remarkable statement, especially when one thinks of Ko-

jève's published disagreement with Strauss, to which I shall turn shortly, over precisely this issue of whether a philosopher can limit himself to persuading a few or must of necessity seek to persuade everyone without preconceived limit.

By no means do I wish to assert that Kojève ended up a Platonist; I am simply suggesting that he may have known himself to be more of a philosopher and less of a wise man than he usually let on. Then of course the next question must necessarily arise: why would he present his thought in such a way? Most philosophers have been satisfied to present themselves as such, without claiming definitive wisdom (although Kojève does note that the Stoics accepted not only the possibility but even the reality of the wise man) (*Introduction to the Reading of Hegel*, in the section "Philosophy and Wisdom," 76). I believe that he had two important reasons. First, he certainly did find Hegel's fundamental philosophic position, as updated by himself (in which task of updating he did not consider that he was discovering a fundamentally new philosophical alternative but perfecting Hegel's), more compelling as a coherent explanation of everything than any other position. His overstatement of this system as definitive knowledge could then be his strongest way of reasserting what philosophy's search is really all about. He may well have judged that such a reassertion was especially important in a present context in which that traditional goal of philosophy's search has been somehow lost, to be replaced by the more limited goal of clarifying the meaning of the words we use, of contemplating the competing world views that have been articulated in the course of history, or of playing the role of methodological conscience for the sciences, including and perhaps especially the social sciences. I would suggest, in other words, that he fully shared in Nietzsche's denunciation of the contemporary loss of a sense of what genuine philosophy really is, expressed in the "We Scholars" section of *Beyond Good and Evil*. Without taking the goal of wisdom seriously—and this must include adequately thinking through what it means truly to assert the possibility of that goal—philosophy could degenerate (and has perhaps already degenerated) into mere "playing with the problems," as Strauss put it in his reply to Kojève's critique (*On Tyranny*, 196).

Kojève's irony is in some sense the exact opposite of the Socratic: the Socratic irony involves claiming not to know, while Socrates' interlocutors have the sneaking suspicion that he knew a lot more than he was willing to let on. Kojèvean irony consists in his advancing the claim of possessing definitive knowledge to an intellectual world in which skepticism and relativism are all the fashion, while at the same time he shows with considerable clarity what still needs to be done toward the full working out of the system of knowledge. And he devoted his leisure to that task of what needed to be done philosophically, above all in the posthumous writings of the 1950s. Of a period in 1956, he wrote that restrictions imposed by his health gave him "more leisure and—in conformity with the ancient model—I devote them to philosophy (which I never entirely abandoned anyway)."[6] Certainly his one-thousand-page *Attempt at a Reasoned History of Pagan Philosophy*, while reaching more people than if it had not been published, addresses the few, not the many. And in the last year of his life, when some German revolutionary students managed to ask Kojève for his guidance on the perennial question of activists or revolutionaries— what is to be done?—his chief advice was to learn Greek. Perhaps Kojève is best understood at the end of the day neither as wise man nor postmodern ironist, but as a philosopher, a philosopher who constantly has in view, and takes with utmost seriousness, philosophy's necessary goal of attaining wisdom.

I turn now from this reflection on the significance of Kojève's changed position on the end of history to an attempt to assess the overall value of his thought. If Hegelianism as updated by Kojève is simply true, then of course the abiding significance of Kojève's philosophical project is perfectly evident and of a very high order of importance, however deeply one must regret its not having been brought to completion. It may be, however, that one has not been able to assure oneself that Kojève's Hegelianism is in fact the definitive philosophical truth, or rather the final (or near-final, because not altogether perfected) system of comprehensive knowledge. In that case, and if the interpretation offered here of Kojèvean irony is correct, I would maintain that the most enduring value of his thought would be its tendency to keep alive the possibility of continued genuine philosophical activity, above all through articulating and affirming the necessary goal to which all genuine philosophy aspires. But I should also like to consider now some more specific aspects of his thinking that emerge from his debate with Strauss and to propose them to the reader as being, perhaps, of enduring significance.

On the most general level, I think (in agreement with Strauss) that Kojève states the case for the distinctively modern philosophical approach more powerfully than anyone else in the twentieth century. Let me begin to elaborate that point by articulating, from the example of Descartes, something basically distinctive of this modern approach. Descartes looked at the philosophical tradition as it had been handed down to him and found it altogether unsatisfactory: after two millennia of philosophical debates, virtually no solid knowledge had been established; the same debates, the same contradictions, the same problems remained unresolved. Could not a new approach, he asked, be found by which progress in knowledge rather than the perpetual repetition of old debates and sterile speculations could take place? Descartes devised a new method with this goal in mind, and in essence thus set Western thought on the path to a new philosophy and a new physics or a new natural science overall, which has produced the degree of mastery over nature that has created the distinctively modern technological world in which we live. But Descartes did not adequately solve all the problems of philosophy; his knowing subject, most notably, was a kind of abstraction that could not give an adequate account of our human being or even of its own possibility of genuinely knowing. Hegel, on a path decisively prepared by Kant, brought this modern approach to its completion.

In his debate with Strauss, Kojève provides an excellent example of this Cartesian-Hegelian imperative to end idle speculations through the establishment of definitive knowledge. He looks at the issue that he and Strauss have been examining, that is, the possibility and desirability of a philosopher's devoting effort to having an effect on politics, and he shows that this issue has been debated back and forth without resolution since the beginning of Western philosophy. Because we are mortal, our time is limited; the philosopher by definition is devoted to seeking the truth; to be able to give effective advice politically (for example, to a tyrant), he would need to devote a great deal of time to the specific details of the actual political order and its situation, and he would in consequence accomplish less as a philosopher. On the level of argument, therefore, this conflict has an unresolvable and even tragic character, and Kojève refers approvingly to Hegel's characterization of *Faust* and *Hamlet* as the only authentic tragedies in the Christian or bourgeois world. But while philosophical debate (as Descartes complained) has not in fact been able to resolve the conflict, history, it turns out, has resolved it in reality through the real effects that the philosophers' thoughts, mediated by intellectuals, have had on political actors (such as Alexander the Great and Napoleon). Accordingly, Hegel's new historical approach, the philosophically coherent understanding of history (including the crucial identification of the Concept with time), puts an end to unresolved philosophical issues and satisfies the characteristically modern demand for definitive answers.

At least some, and perhaps many, of the great modern philosophers were not Christian believers, although they may have made more or less of an effort to disguise that fact. Some of the later modern philosophers, such as Marx, Nietzsche, and Kojève, are explicitly atheistic. And yet for Kojève, following Hegel, the final philosophical truth, while ultimately atheistic, is nonetheless substantially Christian (or if one prefers, Judeo-Christian) in its view of mankind, in its anthropology. Christianity, however erroneous at the time and place it is first enunciated, ends up being true; the secularization of Christianity transforms Christian ideals (errors, longings, illusions at the time of their first formulation) into truths about real human beings. Referring to the word "pagan" in the title of Kojève's *Essai d'une histoire raisonnée de la philosophie païenne* (*Attempt at a Reasoned History of Pagan Philosophy*),

Strauss made a jocular remark welcoming Kojève's returning to the faith of his fathers. The joke has an element of profound truth: Kojève does accept the modern view of Hegel above all because he finds the Judeo-Christian anthropology true, as against the pagan. Two passages in a letter from Kojève to Strauss make this point with especial force.

Responding to his receipt of Strauss's *Natural Right and History* (and while admitting that he has not yet read the entire book), Kojève takes exception to the "Bible quote about the land of the fathers." The quote in question is one of the two biblical passages placed by Strauss as epigraphs to his book, by which he seems to have meant to exemplify "the evidence of those simple experiences regarding right and wrong which are at the bottom of the philosophic contention that there is a natural right" (*Natural Right and History*, 31–32). It reads as follows:

> Naboth the Jezreelite had a vineyard which was in Jezreel, hard by the palace of Ahab king of Samaria. And Ahab spake unto Naboth, saying, Give me thy vineyard, that I may have it for a garden of herbs, because it is near unto my house: and I will give thee for it a better vineyard than it; or, if it seem good to thee, I will give thee the worth of it in money. And Naboth said to Ahab, The Lord forbid it to me, that I should give the inheritance of my fathers unto thee.

Kojève objects that this quote is most problematic: "From it one can of course deduce a condemnation of collectivization in the USSR and elsewhere. But with it one also justifies permanently preserving a Chinese peasant's animal-like starvation-existence (before Mao-Tse-Tung). Etc., etc."[7] Moving on from this issue, which he says is "hardly philosophy," Kojève raises the more fundamental issue of whether the ancient conception of conforming to a given or innate human nature is not incompatible with speaking about "ethics" and "ought":

> For animals, which unquestionably have such a *nature*, are not morally "good" or "evil," but at most *healthy* or *sick*, and *wild* or *trained*. One might therefore conclude that it is precisely *ancient* anthropology that would lead to mass-*training* and *eugenics*.

Kojève, in other words, expresses the view that his modern philosophy is more humane in that it promotes progress in the miserable condition of Chinese peasants and, more philosophically speaking, provides a more solid ground for respect for the human person as free individual than the ancient or pagan philosophical approach can possibly supply. In one way this concern for humaneness and this reservation about "mass-training" may seem quite surprising on the part of someone who knowingly endorsed Stalinist policies that surely included mass-training but also extended to mass murder; but from a Hegelian (or Marxist) standpoint there may arguably be no deep contradiction between humane ends and immensely harsh means, when they are the only or the most efficacious way to move history forward. World history is a slaughter-bench, as we have learned from Hegel himself, and certainly Kojève expressed no disagreement with that; indeed, in his exchange with Strauss, Kojève takes a critical stance toward intellectuals who criticize on the basis of more or less utopian ideals what tyrants are actually doing in order perhaps to move contemporary reality in the progressive direction. Strauss uses two Old Testament quotes to point his readers toward fundamental moral experiences that underlie classical natural right; Kojève, the frank and systematic atheist, rejects Strauss's approach on the grounds of the modern anthropological conception, of Judeo-Christian origin, of the free individuality and the equal dignity of all human beings. Certainly Kojève's position provides anyone with serious matter for reflection on what it might mean to abandon the goals of modern philosophy. His argument that modern philosophy alone can make sense of human freedom should give pause (although not necessarily put a definitive stop) not only to anyone's eager and unreserved enthusiasm for reinstating classical political philosophy but also to any easygoing relativist's confidence that we have no need to secure and no reasonable expectation of securing genuinely rational support for humane goals from philosophy.

Related to their respective adherence to the ancient or the modern approaches to philosophy is another major difference between Strauss and Kojève in regard to the question of the few and the many, of an aristocratic versus a democratic preference, or of an inegalitarian versus an egalitarian tendency. This difference comes to sight in a most interesting manner in the issue that Kojève brings up of how a philosopher needs to interact with others in his society. Strauss and Kojève agree that the philosopher cannot remain satisfied simply with his own thinking in isolation. As Kojève puts it, the subjective certainty of what is considered evident is not enough, even though many philosophers in the tradition, from Plato to Husserl by way of Descartes, have in fact proceeded as though it were. But given the existence of "*illuminati* and 'false prophets' on earth, who never had the least doubt concerning the truth of their 'intuitions' or of the authenticity of the 'revelations' they received in one form or another" (*On Tyranny*, 153), a thinker needs to test his insights in discussion with others, to be sure that he is not deluded or mad. Kojève argues that the philosopher feels the need to try to show the truth of his ideas with as many others as possible, in principle or at the limit, with all others (who are not clinically insane). Thus the philosopher's effort to confirm what he supposes to be his knowledge aims at a universal extension similar to the political man's search for honor or recognition by as many men as possible and so at the limit universally. When Strauss by contrast speaks of a philosopher's being concerned only with the opinion of competent judges, Kojève objects that this distinction is likely in fact to boil down to the view that those who agree with one are the competent, and that others who disagree are held to be proven by that very fact to be incompetent; a real problem arises, given the need for intersubjective confirmation, if one permits oneself to exclude certain interlocutors as incompetent. That distinction, in short, could be used in such a way as to defeat the very purpose of testing one's ideas with others; it leads, according to Kojève, to the formation of sects of fellow believers, within the protective confines of which one no longer truly tests one's ideas against all comers. Furthermore, experience suggests that a small group, though less likely than an individual to be simply mad, can be no less deluded in its beliefs than a single individual may be.

Strauss, by contrast, grasps the other horn of this dilemma. He emphasizes that mere predominance in the numbers of those persuaded cannot be crucial, in isolation from the issue of their competence to judge. Persuading a great many may amount to finding the support of a large mass party, but "the mass party is nothing but a sect with a disproportionately long tail" (*On Tyranny*, 195). Strauss further argues that a philosopher can, like Socrates, resist the tendency to found a sect and to restrict his discussions to any such sect. Thus Kojève favors a more "democratic" or egalitarian-sounding way of dealing with the problem of inter-subjective verification of one's knowledge and Strauss a more "aristocratic" or inegalitarian one. While both see the necessity for the philosopher to test his ideas by engaging in dialogue with others, Kojève notes that such engagement is even more essential if the Hegelian view of philosophy as understanding what emerges from real historical evolution is correct as against the classical notion that one can attain truth in principle at any time and place through gaining access (somehow) to eternal being (of one sort or another). Kojève's more universalistic and egalitarian stance comports with his looking to the outcome of History as the ultimate test or source of truth; Strauss's opposed stance comports with his acceptance of the permanent relevance of natural differences in human types.

A similar difference arises in regard to the understanding of the motive of philosophers and political actors (including tyrants). Strauss emphasizes differences between the philosopher and the political man, most basically that the philosopher by definition is moved by the desire to know whereas the political man is moved by the love of honor. Kojève certainly accepts that the philosopher does have the motivation that Strauss says, but he expresses doubt about whether one can reasonably deny that the philosopher may also, like the political man, be eager to win recognition. Certainly, he says, a philosopher who achieves some success in convincing others of his superior understanding will in fact gain honor. How can we know that that inevitable outcome did not also motivate him? Kojève in fact suggests that the question of what one's deepest inner motivation is only makes sense if one imagines a being who can see inside the human soul even better than an individual may be able to do in regard to himself (that is, a God who sees all in the human heart). But if we can have no access to such knowledge ourselves, we would be closer to the truth to admit that both the philosopher and the political man seek recognition, in connection with his knowledge and his political achievement, respectively. He even adds that, from his observations, intellectuals seem to be if anything more vain than men of action, and he explains that this makes sense. The man of action can point to some objective outcome, independent of people's opinion, as his achievement: "A bridge that does not collapse, a business that makes money, a war won, a state that is strong and prosperous, etc." By contrast, the intellectual's success can only be manifested in the opinions that others have of it (*On Tyranny*, 162n6).

A final key difference between Strauss and Kojève arises from the different status of history in their respective philosophies. Strauss expresses a classical view of the value of utopias in philosophical thinking, as providing understanding of the truly best, which can always help to provide clarity in making practical choices between less perfect alternatives. Kojève, in contrast, is impressed by the uselessness (or even harmfulness) of utopias. For him, a utopia is the elaboration of some ideal by an intellectual in a way that does not and cannot show what the next concrete steps must be to move toward the realization of that ideal. An active political man, including a tyrant, sensibly feels impatience with a critique of his actions that rests on utopian thinking; he will certainly refuse to be guided by a utopian philosopher, and rightly so, in Kojève's view. Since the ultimate object of knowledge for Kojève's Hegelian philosophy is the historical development of mankind, thoughts or ideas such as utopias that do not ultimately produce effective results can reasonably be ignored (as Machiavelli suggested at the beginning of modernity). In connection with this line of thought, Kojève also speaks of tyranny in a way that explicitly welcomes it when major reforms or revolutionary changes are needed, and he notes that when philosophers have in fact made efforts to influence politics, they have, and reasonably enough, generally sought out tyrants to try to advise. We can see here a continuous element of modern political thinking that runs from Machiavelli through Hegel to Marx and Kojève. At the same time, however, it is worth acknowledging that Kojève also has in mind, and indeed mentions, Plato's attempt to advise the tyrant of Syracuse and Aristotle's influence on Alexander the Great.

Continuing to reflect on Kojève's enduring contributions to our thinking, I would turn from these quite fundamental political-philosophical issues dealt with in his debate with Strauss to some more particular areas of his political thought. Here, it seems to me, whether or not one is persuaded by the overall Hegelian argument, Kojève's reflections on the historical unfolding of the universal and homogeneous state offer important ways of thinking about globalization. His discussions of such matters as *droit* (right, justice, and law) and political economy, and of other features of what for him is the working out of the end of history, provide anyone interested in contemporary political life with important matter for thought about what our goals should be and how we can best implement them. His position is of course systematic, left-wing Hegelian, and progressive; but his discussions of political, legal, and economic phenomena are realistic, detailed, and challenging, so as to be of great interest even for someone who may not accept the overall philosophical system.

Regarding authority, for instance, his analysis brings one to reflect on the political importance of tradition (through his rediscovery of the ideal type of the father's authority and his suggestions about the role that such authority might play in politics), as we saw in chapter 3. In his overall discussion of Hegelian dialectic, Kojève balanced the negating, creative, revolutionary aspect of historical change with an insistence on the need for remembrance and tradition: "It is by History which is created, lived, and really remembered as 'tradition' that Man realizes himself or 'appears' as dialectical totality, instead of *annihilating* himself and 'disappearing' by a 'pure' or 'abstract' negation of every given whatsoever, real or thought" (*Introduction to the Reading of Hegel*, 233). In a footnote written in 1946, he elaborated this traditionalist aspect of his political thinking:

> It is in the lack of historical memory (or understanding) that the mortal danger of Nihilism or Skepticism resides, which would negate everything without preserving anything, even in the form of memory. A society that spends its time listening to the radically "nonconformist" Intellectual, who amuses himself by (verbally!) negating any given at all (even the 'sublimated' given preserved in historical remembrance) solely because it is a given, ends up sinking into inactive anarchy and disappearing. Likewise, the Revolutionary who dreams of a "permanent revolution" that negates every type of tradition and takes no account of the concrete past, except to overcome it, necessarily ends up either in the nothingness of social anarchy or in annulling himself physically or politically. Only the Revolutionary who manages to maintain or reestablish the historical tradition, by preserving in a positive memory the given present which he himself has relegated to the past by his negation, succeeds in creating a new historical *World* capable of *existing*. (*Introduction to the Reading of Hegel*, 233)

While one might more likely expect such reflections from a conservative thinker than from Kojève, they by no means display any inconsistency but rather a comprehensively thoughtful treatment of the kind of historical change that can bring forth genuine innovation that endures.

His massive treatment of *droit* (right, law, etc.) sets forth a way of systematically treating that complex and difficult topic that may in the future have productive impact on jurisprudential philosophy, especially in regard to the continued emergence of international law from potentiality into actuality. Since I find his book *Outline of a Phenomenology of Right* so comprehensive and impressive (and in my judgment far more profound than John Rawls' *Theory of Justice*, for example), I was at first puzzled to see how little attention it has drawn so far. I would guess that the explanation lies in the book's style of argument. It is very precise, detailed, and long, and yet at the same time he indicates all kinds of elaborations that would need to be developed but that he is passing over; I suspect that this has discouraged many readers, at least for now.

Kojève's views on political economy and on the importance of overcoming the problem of economic colonialism seem to stand up very well in the light of subsequent events; in fact, his overall position seems more evidently true now than when he stated it in 1957. The weakest point of the argument as he stated it then might seem to be this: whereas Marx in analyzing old-style capitalism viewed the minority as extracting surplus value from the labor of the proletariat, it seemed far from clear that colonialism was extracting surplus value from the *labor* of third-world workers (as distinguished from plundering and exploiting their natural resources). But by now the continued trends of globalization have indeed brought vast numbers of new workers from underdeveloped countries into the global economy, so the possibility of a Marxist analysis of economic colonialism such as Kojève presented has more plausibility on its face. In consequence, the long-run need to mitigate extremes of inequality worldwide is more obvious than ever before. And I would also tend to judge that many measures supported by Kojève have taken root: not so much in the realm of direct foreign aid or revision of the terms of trade to the advantage of underdeveloped countries, but in regard to increased investments by advanced industrialized (now sometimes denominated postindustrialized) countries in the underdeveloped countries, and in the gradual rise of standards of living in these countries.

That the task continues to pose great challenges is surely clear; but that some very substantial gains have been made in the direction that Kojève promoted seems also clear (especially when one thinks of India and China, whose populations comprise so substantial a portion of the peoples whom Kojève considered as not yet industrialized and in need of the assistance of a "giving" rather than a "taking" colonialism). On the other hand, one could certainly make an argument in an opposite direction, that the happy resolution of the basic issues of political economy celebrated by Kojève under the name of "Fordized capitalism" seems anything but definitive. Kojève describes it most briefly as the change from paying workers as little as possible (which produced the problem diagnosed by Marx) to paying workers as much as possible. But the competitive imperative to seek to reduce the cost of all the inputs of production does seem to have its way of reasserting itself so as to threaten previous comfortable resolutions of the problem, as millions of workers who have lost better-paying jobs to outsourcing or downsizing would attest. Outsourcing of jobs to underdeveloped countries, especially when accompanied by the building of factories, of course, can also be viewed as the sort of giving through investing in these countries that Kojève recommends (an example of "giving" colonialism); but on the other hand, it could be viewed as seeking to extract surplus value from laborers abroad (old-style "taking" colonialism). Certainly it reflects the effort by firms to reduce the cost of the labor they need, rather than to remunerate labor as richly as they can. Now all of this is to say that public policy guided by rational analysis of these matters must constantly reexamine the actual facts, adapt appropriately to changes, and so forth. Because Kojève's philosophy is systematic and rationalist, and especially because it affirms the end of history, one's first reaction to this statement of ongoing problems and uncertainties could well be that it argues against his position. But the existence of uncertainties, the need to keep up with changing facts, and the importance of fashioning new adaptations to them do not in any way refute Kojève's position, which is anything but deterministic: the details of how the future will work out remain contingent, although for Kojève, provided that humans do not lapse into stubborn irrationality, the specific policies dealing with the real circumstances that unfold will be rather more the working out of administrative details than the discovery of fundamentally new economic or political orders.

Since the majority of readers of books on twentieth-century political thought are likely to have a special interest in democracy, I turn by way of conclusion to certain of Kojève's discussions that bear on that topic. He leads us toward the basic question of democratic theory through his discussion of the kind of political ruler that to most of us would seem most opposed to democracy, the tyrant. People are likely to think of a tyrant as one who rules by force or terror rather than by recognized authority. This is surely false as stated thus simply, for a man can rule extremely few people by force. Rule by force could only take place in something as small as a family. The tyrant too, like any political leader or chief, must rule in large part by authority: more precisely, some substantial group of people in a society must accept the tyrant's authority, and then indeed he may rule the rest of the society through the use, and the threat to use, the force of that group that he has at his disposal. "The whole question is to know by *whom* this authority is recognized, *who* 'obeys him without constraint'?"[8]

Kojève notes that until relatively recently, the term "tyranny" was used (in a pejorative sense) only when "a minority (guided by an authority it alone recognizes) rules the majority of the citizens by force or 'terror.'" But, he goes on, "recent political experiences, as well as the current polemics between 'Western' and 'Eastern' democrats, have enabled us to provide a more adequate definition of tyranny" (*On Tyranny*, 144–45). According to that definition, a tyranny (in the morally neutral sense) exists when a fraction of the citizens (whether minority or majority) imposes its ideas and actions (under the leadership of one whose authority members of that fraction recognize) on another fraction that rejects those ideas and that authority, and does so without persuading or coming to compromise with the other fraction but by relying on force or terror to prevail. If this is tyranny, what, then, is democracy? From Kojève's reference to Eastern and Western democrats, it appears that he is willing to use the term quite broadly: the term would certainly apply, I think, to any society's political governance that is supported by a majority of the citizens, and perhaps to one that claims (more or less plausibly) the support of a majority or even that claims to be working for the interests of the majority. We (in the developed countries) are virtually all democrats now. A tyranny, as Kojève uses the term, could certainly be the means, and might indeed be the necessary means, for establishing democracy in the first place. He explicitly states, following Machiavelli among others, that a tyrant is needed for major structural change or revolution. In a well-functioning established democracy, at the limit, all citizens would recognize the governing authority, and so little or no tyrannical element would remain.

Any tyrant—and the tyrant Hiero exemplifies this in Xenophon's dialogue—would, in his pursuit of recognition or honor, wish to be recognized as the political authority by as large a proportion of his citizens as possible, and at the limit, of course, by all his citizens. In Kojève's understanding, the advice that Xenophon's Simonides gives to Hiero to that end is utopian (and therefore Hiero makes no response to it). But for Kojève, in the course of history it has come to pass that a previously utopian-sounding way to improve tyranny is now commonplace. His reference to some of the policies recommended by Simonides as establishing "'Stakhanovite' emulation" and "organizing a State police" reminds one of his favorable view of the modern tyrant, Stalin. At this stage of history, the modern tyrant, in working to implement an ideologically guided project (derived by intellectuals at some distance from an original philosophical source), does actually aim at securing the support of all his citizens, at having his authority recognized by them all. The modern tyrant thus can be understood, in Kojève's judgment, to be realistically working toward something like historically progressive democracy.

Democracy for Kojève did not seem necessarily to involve specific constitutional forms or institutions, such as majority rule (which itself, of course, is subject to quite varied interpretations and implementations). In his book *Authority*, we recall, he argued that a faction's being a majority does not as such give it authority over the minority, any more than the converse; somewhat related to that point, he takes election and lot to be basically the same mode of choice. What is it then that would make a political order meaningfully democratic? Kojève's implicit answer would seem to be that a government is democratic when its authority is recognized by the bulk of the people, it includes as full citizens as much of the population as possible, and it acts for their well-being.

In his "Latin Empire," Kojève refers several times in one paragraph to democracy, in section III on "The Idea of the Latin Empire." Here he is concerned with what democratic theory might be able to develop to apply to the new political entity that would embrace a number of related, affiliated nations. He suggests that the spiritual and psychic kinship of the Latin nations would help to assure to their relations "that character of liberty, equality and fraternity without which there is no true democracy." He suggests further that the greater resources of an empire, as compared to the narrower confines of a nation, might permit going beyond the sterile and paralyzing opposition of Left and of Right. He concludes:

> Finally, the organization of the Latin Empire, which would be something essentially other than the Anglo-Saxon Commonwealth or the Soviet Union, would present democratic political thought with new (*inédits*) problems that would allow it finally to go beyond its traditional ideology, which is adapted only to *national* cadres and is consequently anachronistic. Perhaps it is in determining the relationships between Nations within an Empire (and at the limit,—within Humanity) that democracy will once more have something to say to the contemporary world. ("L'Empire Latin," 105)

Democracy, then, for Kojève involves the well-known liberty, equality, fraternity, whose real existence in a political society depends (for now) on shared culture and traditions. The details of working out institutions and constitutions for democratic functioning in new contexts—the interim stage of empires, to be followed ultimately by the universal and homogeneous state— remains a matter for practical statesmen of the future to work out.

In sum, Kojève held to an uncommonly systematic philosophical doctrine (or even *System of Knowledge*) that made an unusual and strong claim about the attainment of the end of history. Nonetheless, the future is far from determined in all its political, administrative, and juridical details, but is subject to contingent paths of events. Even one who accepts the Kojèvean-Hegelian political philosophy must act (in a practical, if no longer in a world-historically revolutionary way) with full knowledge and adequate consideration of all the particular circumstances of the time and place. A year or so after Kojève's death, Raymond Aron met with a group of a few American students[9] and, among other topics, reminisced a bit about Kojève. He told us with some amusement how, for all of Kojève's definitive Hegelian philosophy and confident affirmation of the end of history, when an international crisis of one sort or another was brewing, Kojève would telephone Aron to find out what he thought was really going on.

NOTES

1. Shadia Drury, in *Alexandre Kojève: The Roots of Postmodern Politics* (New York: St. Martin's Press, 1994), makes interesting and often convincing arguments for the influence of Kojève on leading postmodernist thinkers, but her argument about Kojève's own position often fails to persuade in that it appears to emerge more from a preconceived judgment than from an attentive reading of his texts.

2. Michael S. Roth suggests that the later Kojève's "posthistorical ironic philosophy of history has become a dominant mode of what today is called postmodern cultural criticism." Since Roth recognizes Kojève's continued "commitment to the possibilities of self-consciousness" and that "his discourse was still pointed toward the creation of a consciousness that could initiate political action," Kojève would not have become postmodern himself (Roth 1995, 152, 154, 160).

3. Letter of September 11, 1957. *On Tyranny*, 291.

4. Michael S. Roth seems to me on the right track in arguing that the later Kojève's "pedagogic effort to establish a Hegelian self-consciousness for our times must be read *against* his nihilistic description of the animalization of man" (Roth 1988, 142).

5. Letter of March 29, 1962. *On Tyranny*, 307–308.

6. Letter of June 8, 1956. *On Tyranny*, 265.

7. Letter of October 29, 1953. *On Tyranny*, 262.

8. *On Tyranny*, 144. The question of distinguishing tyranny from governments that are more respectable has, of course, a very long history. Kojève's discussion, especially since it takes place in the context of his critical review of a book about Xenophon's *Hiero or Tyrannicus*, may properly remind one of Alcibiades' questioning of Pericles about tyranny versus lawful government in Xenophon's *Memorabilia* I.2.

9. I was one of the group. Allan Bloom had arranged the meeting with M. Aron.

Epilogue: Philosophy, Politics— and Espionage?

In November of 1999, the most prestigious French newspaper, *Le Monde*, published a story by Pascal Ceaux containing the allegation that for thirty years Kojève had been an agent for the KGB. The newspaper's overall report, dealing with the KGB's penetration of France, was occasioned by the publication in England of *The Mitrokhin Archive*, coauthored by the British historian Christopher Andrew and the former KGB official Vasiliy Mitrokhin (since published in the United States as *The Sword and the Shield: Secret History of the KGB*). In a chapter about France, the book indicated that some fifty KGB agents had been active in French political, technological, business, and intellectual circles. The French counterintelligence agency, le Directoire du Surveillance du Territoire (DST), had put together in 1982–1983 a three-page synthesis of information, with the title "L'espionnage de l'Est et la gauche" ("Espionage by the East and the Left") regarding KGB agents in France. Reporters at *Le Monde* had seen a copy of this DST paper and had noted considerable overlap with information published in *The Mitrokhin Archive* regarding a few political and other figures. Kojève, according to *Le Monde*'s report, was named as having worked for the KGB for thirty years (presumably from 1938 until his death in 1968) in the DST account, but there is nothing in the published Andrew Mitrokhin book that would seem to refer to him.

What is one to make of this story? The DST paper, according to *Le Monde*'s account, provides a synthetic overview without presenting any of the evidence for its assertions. The only particular assertion made regarding Kojève is that he played an important role in the context of links between Charles Hernu (a former minister of defense) and the KGB. Certainly one must say that, without the DST's releasing its account and the sources on which it is based, one cannot tell what the claim about Kojève means. At one extreme, one could imagine that he acted as an information source or agent of influence for the KGB. At the other extreme, given his publicly stated support for the Soviet experiment and even for Stalin's actions, one can well imagine that the KGB listed him as one of theirs, as an agent of influence, even without having established any specific relationship with Kojève. *The Mitrokhin Archive* makes clear that the KGB *Résidence* in Paris, like many another government bureaucracy or political individual, often claimed more credit for efforts and accomplishments than it in fact deserved.

Reaction to this spy scandal varied widely, as one might well expect. In *The Daily Telegraph* of London, Daniel Johnson's article of 2 October was headlined "Europe's greatest traitor" and seemed to exult in the alleged fact that "this miraculous mandarin turns out to have been a malevolent mole. Nobody of this eminence has ever been exposed as a traitor on this scale before." In *Le Monde* of 4 October, Edmond Ortigues, under the heading "Pour l'honneur d'Alexandre Kojève" ("For Alexandre Kojève's honor"), argued on the basis of his personal knowledge of Kojève going back to 1951 that the charge was absurd, that it was psychologically impossible for him to have been seduced by the KGB, that his political orientation was not at all pro-Soviet but solidly pro-Europe, and that his statements in praise of Stalin or in regret at his death were ironical.

The most detailed, thoughtful, and nuanced reflection on this charge of espionage was presented eight days after it had appeared by Kojève's biographer, Dominique Auffret, in *Le Monde* of 24 September. Auffret reports that he was not altogether surprised at the published report. He had heard a DST informant make a similar assertion about Kojève's connection to the KGB on the phone to Annie Kriegel (a historian of communism) shortly after the publication of his own biography of Kojève. Furthermore, Auffret thought that some of the difficulties he had encountered in researching the biography might be explained by the knowledge or at least the strong suspicion on the part of some of those who were close to Kojève of some such KGB connection. Auffret drew attention to the fact that specifics of the allegation are unknown. We know for certain only that the DST had a dossier on Kojève, but of course the DST opened many dossiers on many people during the Cold War and had several reasons to open one on Kojève: his Russian origin, his reputation as a leftist Hegelian or Marxist, and after the war his position as a high government counselor on economic and commercial matters. Without knowing anything of the contents of that dossier, however, one can only speculate on what the facts of the matter may have been.

Auffret vividly sketched, given what we know of Kojève's character and thought, the utter implausibility of imagining him slavishly following orders from the KGB or the policy of the Kremlin. In Kojève's belief, Stalin was not aiming at worldwide dominion but at strengthening his Slavo-Soviet empire, while Kojève himself, throughout his life in public service, was deeply concerned with and actively engaged in building a viable European empire (with an important role for France) from the ashes left after the war. Auffret offers the following hypothesis as worthy of serious consideration, if it should turn out that a link between Kojève and the KGB did indeed exist: that "Kojève sought to use the KGB to his ends, and perhaps even in perfect agreement with the French governments." Auffret evokes Kojève's acceptance (in the 1942 manuscript *Authority*) of the idea that it might be necessary, if the Nazis emerged victorious from the war, to work with them with a view to preparing against them the post-Nazi world, although there is absolutely no indication in speech, writing, or deed of any sympathy for Nazism on Kojève's part. "Still less should one suppose that Kojève, if he had been the agent of the KGB reputed by the DST, could have 'rallied' to Soviet Russia as a 'traitor.'"

Given the dearth of factual information about Kojève's alleged relation to the KGB, Auffret's comments seem to me about as reasonable as one could make. I should simply like to add, on the hypothesis of Kojève's having worked for the KGB in some way, a broader reflection on its possible significance in the two different periods of Kojève's stance toward the end of history. For the earlier, activist-Marxist Kojève, who went so far as to describe his Hegel interpretation as a work of political propaganda, it is easy to understand how he might have chosen to work for the KGB. Especially in the circumstances of the late 1930s, with displays of weakness from Great Britain and France in the face of Fascist and Nazi aggression, it is in no way surprising that a leftist thinker would look to the Soviet Union—even Stalin's Soviet Union—for hope for the future. Certainly the Marxist-Hegelian view of history gives no support to moral standards (of truthfulness, say, or fair-dealing) on any basis apart from their place in the progressive pattern of historical development. In a thoroughly Machiavellian mode, actions are justified when they succeed in moving history forward; they meet with effective blame only when they fail. In this philosophical perspective, as John Harington wrote, "Treason doth never prosper. What's the reason? / For if it prosper, none dare call it treason." For someone who held that the Soviet Union was the locus of the final revolution to advance the rational end of history, what scruple would oppose one's promoting the interests of humanity in the revolution by putting one's influence or information at the service of the KGB?

The situation looks more complex when, a few years after the war, Kojève came to believe both that Hegel had been right about history's ending in 1806 and that the United States was further along toward that end of history than the Soviets. Why might he have worked for the KGB then? The answer could turn on any number of contingencies unknown to us. One set of contingencies might be personal: being blackmailed, for instance, or otherwise not permitted to abandon an existing relationship. Another contingency might be a combined political and personal one: given all the uncertainties of political life, always but especially in the middle third of the twentieth century, a prudent concern for one's own interests might recommend keeping a foot in both camps. A third possible explanation could be the hypothesis proposed by Auffret: Kojève might have kept a KGB connection and put it to use somehow in connection with carrying out his own political purposes.

It is important in all this to recall the place of contingency in Kojève's understanding of politics. When we think chiefly of his claims about the end of history, we can easily overlook how many things of great moment remain in his view contingent. Kojève often restated his conviction that one cannot know the future, that the philosopher is not a prophet. He was perfectly explicit and clear about this in his earlier period: the future end of history, being as yet unreal, is subject to the fundamental contingency that it may never exist; the paths to that contingent future end of history are no less undetermined in advance and hence matters of contingency. (That, by the way, is why Kojève's change from the view that the Soviet Union was leading the way to the end of history to the conviction that the United States' post-Ford political economy had progressed further is very interesting indeed, but not a philosophically fundamental change in thinking.)

From the later Kojève's argument that history was over, it does indeed follow that one aspect of contingency in human history is also over: no new political order can emerge that is both fundamentally different and rational. But immense contingencies remain, which from most people's commonsense perspective are of very great importance and interest. Just what path will the world follow from nation-states via empires toward the universal and homogeneous state? What will these empires be? Which ones will emerge and prosper and which will fail? How will they be governed? Through what changes will movement toward a universal and homogeneous state take place? What kinds of families, what kinds of laws of property, will prevail in the future? Beyond these questions, the answers to which are not known in advance, the place of contingency in human affairs means that there is no guarantee that irrationality may not break out to obstruct the rational elaboration of the end of history at any conjuncture along the way.

Bearing these considerations regarding contingency in mind, we can more readily understand how the later Kojève's activity devoted to the construction of a European empire could have engaged his interest no less than his philosophical project of updating Hegel. The ironies abound. Kojève often spoke of his practical activity as administration of the details of the end of history; but in fact, the political contingencies seem so great as to make even so-called posthistorical administration deeply interesting. Kojève likewise spoke of philosophy as being over with Hegel's achievement, and hence of wisdom as being in principle available. But in fact, as we have seen, Hegelian wisdom in Kojève's view still needs a lot of work, and its updating and completion were the unattained goal of his philosophical efforts. A final irony: Kojève, who wrote (in his debate with Strauss) about the impossibility of a genuine philosopher's being a truly successful statesman, ended up dividing his time between both activities.

Bibliography

PUBLISHED WRITINGS BY ALEXANDRE KOJÈVE

"L'Action politique des philosophes." *Critique*, nos. 41/42 (1950): 46–55, 138–155. [English translation as "Tyranny and Wisdom."]

L'Athéisme. Trans. Nina Avanoff, ed. Laurent Bibard. Paris: Éditions Gallimard, 1998. [Originally written in 1931.]

"Autonomie et dépendance de la Conscience-de-soi: Maîtrise et Servitude." In *Mesures*, 14 January 1939. [Used as the first section, 11–34, of *Introduction à la Lecture de Hegel* and in English translation in *Introduction to the Reading of Hegel*, 3–30.]

"Le Concept et le Temps." *Deucalion*, no. 5 (October 1955): 11–20.

Le Concept, le Temps et le Discours: Introduction au Système du Savoir. Présentation par Bernard Hesbois. Paris: Éditions Gallimard, 1990. [Originally written in 1952– .]

"Correspondance with Leo Strauss [1934–1962]." In *On Tyranny*. Revised and expanded edition, ed. Victor Gourevitch and Michael S. Roth. Chicago: University of Chicago Press, 2000.

Critique of two books by Gaston Fessard: *Pax nostra: Examen de conscience international* (Paris: Grasset, 1936) and *La Main tendue? Le dialogue catholique-communiste est-il possible?* (Paris: Grasset, 1937). Written 1937 or 1938 for *Recherches philosophiques*, which ceased to appear. In Jarczyk, Gwendolin, and Pierre-Jean Labarrière, *De Kojève à Hegel: 150 ans de pensée hégélienne en France* (Paris: Édition Albin Michel, 1996), 131–136.

"Le Dernier Monde Nouveau." *Critique*, nos. 111/112 (1956): 702–708.

"The Emperor Julian and His Art of Writing." Trans. James H. Nichols, Jr. In *Ancients and Moderns: Essays on the Tradition of Political Philosophy in Honor of Leo Strauss*, ed. Joseph Cropsey. New York: Basic Books, 1964.

"L'Empire Latin: Esquisse d'une Doctrine de la Politique Française (1945)" (text slightly abridged). *La Règle du Jeu*, no. 1 (mai 1990). English translation of the complete manuscript text, "Outline of a Doctrine of French Policy (August 27,

1945)" by Erik de Vries in *Policy Review* (2004), available at http://www.policy review.org/aug04/kojeve_print.html.

"Entretien avec Gilles Lapouge: 'Les Philosophes ne m'intéressent pas, je cherche des sages.'" *La Quinzaine littéraire* 53 (1–15 July 1968): 18–20.

Esquisse d'une Phénoménologie du Droit: Exposé Provisoire. Paris: Éditions Gallimard, 1981. English translation: *Outline of a Phenomenology of Right*. Ed. and trans. Bryan-Paul Frost and Robert Howse. Lanham, MD: Rowman & Littlefield, 2000. [Originally written in 1943.]

Essai d'une histoire raisonnée de la philosophie païenne. [Originally written in 1953–1955.]

Vol. 1: *Les Présocratiques*. Paris: Éditions Gallimard, 1968.

Vol. 2: *Platon et Aristote*. Paris: Éditions Gallimard, 1972.

Vol. 3: *La Philosophie Héllénistique et le Néoplatonisme*. Paris: Éditions Gallimard, 1973.

"Hegel, Marx, et le christianisme." *Critique*, nos. 3/4 (1946): 339–366. English translation: "Hegel, Marx, and Christianity." Trans. Hilail Gilden. *Interpretation: A Journal of Political Philosophy* 1, no. 1 (Summer 1970): 21–42.

L'Idée du Déterminisme dans la Physique Classique et la Physique Moderne. Présentation par Dominique Auffret. Paris: Le Livre de Poche, 1990. [Originally written in 1932.]

Introduction à la Lecture de Hegel. Ed. Raymond Queneau. Paris: Éditions Gallimard, 1947 (second edition, 1962). An English translation of about half of the French text is available as *Introduction to the Reading of Hegel*. Ed. Allan Bloom, trans. James H. Nichols, Jr. New York: Basic Books, 1969. [It has been reissued by Cornell University Press, Agora Edition paperbacks, 1980.] The most important part omitted from this English translation is the second appendix: "L'idée de la mort dans la philosophie de Hegel." An English translation by Joseph Carpino, "The Idea of Death in the Philosophy of Hegel," is available in *Interpretation: A Journal of Political Philosophy* 3, nos. 2/3 (Winter 1973): 114–156.

Kant. Paris: Éditions Gallimard, 1973. [Originally written 1953–1955.]

"Kolonialismus in europäischer Sicht." In *Schmittiana*, Volume VI, 126–140. Berlin: Duncker & Humboldt, 1998. [Lecture originally delivered in 1957.] An English translation by Erik De Vries, "Colonialism from a European Perspective," is available together with Kojève-Carl Schmitt correspondence in *Interpretation: A Journal of Political Philosophy* 29, no. 1 (Fall 2001): 91–130.

Letter to Tran-Duc-Thao, October 7, 1948. In Jarczyk and Labarrière, *De Kojève à Hegel*, 64–66.

"La Métaphysique religieuse de Vladimir Soloviev (1)" and "La Métaphysique religieuse de Vladimir Soloviev (2)." *Revue d'histoire et de philosophie religieuses* 14 (1934): 534–554, and 15 (1935): 110–152.

La Notion de l'Autorité. Ed. François Terré. Paris: Éditions Gallimard, 2004. [Originally written in 1942.]

"L'origine chrétienne de la science moderne." *Mélanges Alexandre Koyré*, Volume 2. Paris, 1964. An English translation, "The Christian Origin of Modern Science," by David R. Lachterman appeared in *St. John's Review* 35, no. 1 (Winter 1984): 22–26.

"Les Peintures Concrètes de Kandinsky." *Revue de Métaphysique et de Morale* 90, no. 2 (1985): 149–171. [Originally written in 1936.]

"Les Romans de la Sagesse." *Critique*, no. 60 (1952): 387–397.

"Tyranny and Wisdom." In *On Tyranny*. Revised and expanded edition including the Strauss-Kojève correspondence, ed. Victor Gourevitch and Michael S. Roth. Chicago: University of Chicago Press, 2000.

"Was ist Dialektik?" *Deutsche Zeitschrift für Philosophie* 50, no. 2 (2002): 317–329. [Lecture delivered in 1967.]

BOOKS AND ARTICLES ABOUT KOJÈVE

Andrew, Christopher, and Vasiliy Mitrokhin. *The Sword and the Shield: The Mitrokhin Archive and the Secret History of the KGB*. New York: Basic Books, 1999.

Aron, Raymond. *The Committed Observer: Interviews with Jean-Louis Missika and Dominique Wolton*. Trans. James and Marie McIntosh. Chicago: Regnery-Gateway, 1983. Translation of *Le Spectateur Engagé: Cinquante Ans de Reflexion Politique*. Paris: Éditions Julliard, 1981.

——. *Mémoires: 50 ans de réflexion politique*. Paris: Éditions Juillard, 1983. English translation: *Memoirs: Fifty Years of Political Reflection*. Trans. George Holoch. New York: Holmes & Meier, 1990.

Auffret, Dominique. *Alexandre Kojève: La philosophie, l'Etat, la fin de l'Histoire*. Paris: Editions Grasset & Fasquelle, 1990.

——. "Alexandre Kojève: du trompe-l'oeil au vertige." *Le Monde*, 24 September 1999, 18.

Bloom, Allan. "Editor's Introduction." *Introduction to the Reading of Hegel*, vii–xii.

Butler, Judith. *Subjects of Desire: Hegelian Reflections in Twentieth-Century France*. New York: Columbia University Press, 1987 (paperback edition, 1999).

Ceaux, Pascal. "La DST avait identifié plusieurs agents du KGB parmi lesquels le philosophe Alexandre Kojève." *Le Monde*, 16 September 1999, 14.

Cooper, Barry. *The End of History: An Essay in Hegelian Interpretation*. Toronto: University of Toronto Press, 1984.

Cropsey, Joseph, ed. *Ancients and Moderns: Essays on the Tradition of Political Philosophy in Honor of Leo Strauss*. New York: Basic Books, 1964.

Descombes, Vincent. *Modern French Philosophy*. Trans. L. Scott-Fox and J. M. Harding. Cambridge: Cambridge University Press, 1980. Translation of *Le Même et L'Autre: quarante-cinq ans de philosophie française (1933–1978)*. Paris: Les Editions de Minuit, 1979.

Devlin, F. Roger. *Alexandre Kojève and the Outcome of Modern Thought*. Lanham, MD: University Press of America, 2004.

Drury, Shadia B. *Alexandre Kojève: The Roots of Postmodern Politics*. New York: St. Martin's Press, 1994.

Frachon, Alain. "Le KGB avait tissé un vaste réseau d'influence en France." *Le Monde*, 19 September 1999, 14.

Frost, Bryan-Paul. "A Critical Introduction to Alexandre Kojève's *Esquisse d'une Phénoménologie du Droit*." *The Review of Metaphysics* 53, no. 3 (March 1999): 595–640.

Fukuyama, Francis. "The End of History?" *The National Interest*, no. 16 (Summer 1989): 3–18.

———. *The End of History and the Last Man*. New York: Free Press, 1993.

Gourevitch, Victor. "Philosophy and Politics." *The Review of Metaphysics* 22, nos. 1/2 (September and December 1968): 58–84, 281–328.

Howse, Robert. "Kojève's Latin Empire." *Policy Review* (August 2004).

Jarczyk, Gwendoline, and Pierre-Jean Labarière. *De Kojève à Hegel: 150 ans de pensée hégélienne en France*. Paris: Édition Albin Michel, 1996.

Johnson, Daniel. "Europe's Greatest Traitor." *The Daily Telegraph*, 2 October 1999.

Lilla, Mark. *The Reckless Mind: Intellectuals in Politics*. New York: New York Review of Books Press, 2001.

Moss, M. E. *Giovanni Gentile: Mussolini's Fascist Philosopher*. New York: Peter Lang, 2004.

Nietzsche, Friedrich. *Beyond Good and Evil*. Trans. Walter Kaufman. New York: Random House, 1966.

Ortigues, Edmond. "Pour l'honneur d'Alexandre Kojève." *Le Monde*, 4 October 1999, 17.

Patri, Aimé. "Dialectique du Maître et de l'Esclave." *Le Contrat Social* 5, no. 4 (July–August 1961).

Poster, Mark. *Existential Marxism in Postwar France: From Sartre to Althusser*. Princeton, NJ: Princeton University Press, 1975.

Queneau, Raymond. *The Sunday of Life*. Trans. Barbara Wright. New York: New Directions Books, 1977.

Riley, Patrick. "Introduction to the Reading of Alexandre Kojève." *Political Theory* 9, no. 1 (February 1981): 5–48.

Rosen, Stanley. *Hermeneutics as Politics*. New York: Oxford University Press, 1987.

Roth, Michael S. "A Note on Kojève's *Phenomenology of Right*." *Political Theory* 11 (1983): 447–450.

———. Review of Barry Cooper, *The End of History: An Essay on Modern Hegelianism*. *Political Theory* 13 (1985).

———. "A Problem of Recognition: Alexandre Kojève and the End of History." *History and Theory* 21, no. 3 (1985): 293–306.

———. *Knowing and History: Appropriations of Hegel in Twentieth-Century France*. Ithaca, NY: Cornell University Press, 1988.

———. "Natural Right and the End of History: Leo Strauss and Alexandre Kojève." *Revue de Métaphysique et de Morale*, no. 3 (1991): 407–422.

———. *The Ironist's Cage: Memory, Trauma, and the Construction of History*. New York: Columbia University Press, 1995.

Strauss, Leo. "Restatement on Xenophon's *Hiero*." In *On Tyranny*. Revised and expanded edition including the Strauss-Kojève correspondence, ed. Victor Gourevitch and Michael S. Roth. Chicago: University of Chicago Press, 2000.

———. *Natural Right and History*. Chicago: University of Chicago Press, 1953.

Index

143

About the Author

James H. Nichols, Jr., is professor of political science at Claremont McKenna College and Avery Fellow at Claremont Graduate University. His research and teaching deal with political philosophy. His publications include *Epicurean Political Philosophy: On the* De rerum natura *of Lucretius*; translations with introduction, notes, and interpretative essays of Plato's *Gorgias* and *Phaedrus*; and articles on pragmatism, human rights, Plato's view of philosophic education, liberalism, and political economy. His current research deals with the Roman imperial historian Tacitus.

Printed in Great Britain
by Amazon.co.uk, Ltd.,
Marston Gate.